GEF
THE
TALKING MONGOOSE
THE "EIGHTH WONDER OF THE WORLD"

D1607330

INCLUDES:
THE HAUNTING OF
CASHEN'S GAP
BY HARRY PRICE & R.S. LAMBERT

TIM R. SWARTZ
WITH ADDITIONAL MATERIAL BY:
TIMOTHY GREEN BECKLEY, HERCULES INVITICUS,
PAUL DALE ROBERTS

GEF THE TALKING MONGOOSE

The "Eighth Wonder of the World"

Includes:

The Haunting of Cashen's Gap – A Modern "Miracle"

Inner Light/Global Communications

Gef The Talking Mongoose - The "Eight Wonder of the World"
By Tim R. Swartz

Addition Material by: Timothy Green Beckley - Hercules Invictus - Paul Dale Roberts

Includes the complete editon: *The Haunting of Cashen's Gap - A Modern "Miracle" by* Harry Price and R.S. Lambert
Originally Published 1936 by Methuen & CO. LTD. London

Published in the United States of America by Inner Light/Global Communications, PO Box 753 - New Brunswick, NJ 08903

Staff Members:
Timothy G. Beckley, Publisher
Carol Ann Rodriguez, Assistant to the Publisher
Sean Casteel, General Associate Editor
Tim R. Swartz, Graphics and Editorial Consultant
William Kern, Editorial and Art Consultant

www.ConspiracyJournal.com

Order Hot Line: 1-732-602-3407

PayPal: MrUFO8@hotmail.com

CONTENTS

OF COURSE A MONGOOSE CAN'T TALK!
By Timothy Green Beckley

Some stories just stick with you.

There are some stories you want to read over and over again.

In the world of unexplained, paranormal, phenomena, the story of Gef the talking mongoose has no parallel. The account has been around for a century or more and you would think that in this age of technical enlightenment it would be laughed and snickered at so much that no researcher worth their salt would dare bring up this outrageous account.

On a scale of one to ten in the ranks of Fortiana (i.e. with respect to Charles Fort, grandfather of the supernatural) I would have to give it a solid nine for its overall appeal and its refusal to go away with the passing of time.

Yes Gef could talk!

What else can be said? There is solid evidence that those who were at the center of this story were not responsible for creating a hoax.. Witnesses came from far and wide and heard the mongoose talk. True to most he was nothing more than a vague shadow on the wall, but they knew it was not the little girl throwing her voice. Long before the day of tape recorders, there was no such device planted in the wall, nor was this a stunt caused by short wave or a ham operator.

Harry Price was one of the most respected men in psychic research at the time. He devoted a large book to the subject of his investigation. The book is very rare and collectors are paying a thousand dollars for a copy, while you can read its full content here, unabridged and with additional updated material from some of the masters of the new science of parapsychology.

There is even a Gef The Talking Mongoose group on Facebook that you can join and share information. This book wouldn't be in your hands – or on your ebook device – if it wasn't for an anonymous "donor" whose husband scanned the original Price book for us.

Maybe Gef has a descendant out there somewhere. In which case come and talk to us. We'll do our best to keep your secret – no ordinary rodent masquerading as a talking mongoose need apply.

mrufo8@hotmail.com

Subscribe for free to our YouTube channel – Mr UFOs Secret Files

Gef even has his own beer by Bushy's Ale of Man. Called "Dalby Spook," it is described as "spicy, full bodied, straw coloured bitter."

Below: A "Gef-like" animal depicted in an ancient stone carving.

9

The Eighth Wonder of the World
By Tim R. Swartz

I first read about Gef the talking mongoose at a fairly early age from a paperback copy of Nandor Fodor's book *"Between Two Worlds."* The bizarre tale of the "Dalby Spook" was unlike any ghost story or paranormal weirdness that I had run across before. At the age of 12 I was already well-versed in tales of UFOs, poltergeists, imps-fairies and cryptid creatures. But Gef was so unique that when other stories had faded over time, it remained fresh in my mind. The legend of Gef is so unusual that books, discussions and conferences about him are still taking place – almost 90 years since he first made his appearance. In fact, there is even a song written about him by Lemon Demon called "Eighth Wonder."

The story of Gef begins on the Isle of Man, an island in the Irish Sea between Great Britain and Ireland. On a small, isolated farm on the west side of the island, James Irving and his family found themselves in the crosshairs of a series of increasingly strange events that would dominate their lives for years to come.

James "Jim" Irving, an educated man, had previously been a traveling piano salesman, and although the farm was his retirement project, it was proving insufficient to support his wife, Margaret, and their young daughter, Voirrey. Voirrey was not the Irving's only child; however, the two older children, Elsie and Gilbert were already grown and living on their own in Liverpool and London when Jim, Margaret and Voirrey moved to Man. The farm was called Doarlish Cashen — Manx Gaelic for "Cashen's Gap." The farm was completely different from their previous life in England. There were no neighbors nearby, nor was there a telephone or electricity.

Gef made his first appearance on Sept. 13, 1931. According to Jim Irving, he first saw a small, weasel-like animal in his farmyard that could bark like a dog and meows like a cat. Even more amazing, when Irving made other barnyard animal noises, the little animal would repeat the sounds back immediately. It wasn't long before the Irving's became aware that this creature had found its way into their home, announcing its presence with random scratches, rustling and general activity between the walls and the matchwood paneling.

At first they supposed that their home had been invaded by rats and other pests and attempted to trap them, unsuccessfully. Jim made a last-ditch attempt by growling like a dog at the pests, only to hear something growl back. Irving realized that this was the animal he had previously seen outside. Whatever it was, it proved to be a talented mimic. It would repeat Irving's imitations of various animals and birds, and soon he had only to name an animal and it would promptly respond with the appropriate sounds. At other times it made a gurgling sound like a baby that soon changed into actual words.

Irving would later write: "Something was happened that made us speechless with amazement and apprehension. This strange animal – whatever it was – made gurgling sounds like a baby trying to talk for the first time! It sounded like this – 'DOMADOMADOMA-BLUMBLUMBLUM.'"

The tale of Gef the Talking Mongoose has even been immortalized as a graphic novel from artist Andy Glass.

Gef Learns to Speak

Voirrey was fascinated by their new guest. She would ask the creature to repeat nursery rhymes and it obliged in a clear, high-pitched, voice. At first the Irving's referred to the animal as "Jack," but soon it told the Irving's that he preferred to be known as Gef, which he spelled out as G-E-F. Gef said that he had been born in Delhi, India in 1852 and was brought to the island twenty years earlier when a farmer had imported mongooses to the island hoping to curb the local rabbit population. Gef also said that he could always understand human speech, but it wasn't until Jim Irving started talking to it that it learned to speak as well.

Rumors across the island swirled that Voirrey was actually fooling everyone by hoaxing Gef – a viewpoint also made by a reporter for the *Manchester Daily Dispatch*. Her classmates said that she entertained them with spot on imitations of animal noises. Manx Radio in 2001 featured Kathleen Green, an old friend of Voirrey's. In the program, *A Time to Remember*, Green told David Callister that Voirrey had a talent at being able to throw her voice.

However, the claim that Voirrey was fooling everyone by "throwing her voice" is absurd. There is no such thing as "throwing ones voice." Ventriloquism works by using the art of misdirection. Stage ventriloquists use a doll that becomes the focus of the audience's attention. When a ventriloquist throws his voice, he simply muffles his voice, so that it appears to be coming from somewhere else, like inside a box. The ventriloquist then directs the audience's attention to the box.

This is not to say that Voirrey probably didn't at times imitate Gef's voice. Practically every poltergeist case that centers on children there are instances where the child is seen to throw something or bang on a wall if they think that they are not being observed. Voirrey was probably guilty of doing this when Gef would become stubborn and refuse to make an appearance. But it is unlikely that Voirrey could have managed to keep such a long, drawn out hoax going for as long as it did.

Was Gef A Poltergeist?

Right from the beginning investigators speculated that Gef was a haunting of some kind – possibly a poltergeist. Gef could produce knocks and raps all over the house practically simultaneously. He was also fond of throwing things at the Irving's and their guests from the cracks in the paneling. As well, Gef claimed to be able to travel all over the island and repeat various conversations that he had overheard. He was also had a rich vocabulary of swear words and loved to sing songs that were unknown to his hosts. These antics are very similar to traditional poltergeist pranks and even Jim Irving thought at times that Gef was more than an just "extra clever mongoose."

Irving was under the impression that Gef could become invisible and even change his shape. On at least two occasions, in a letter to Captain James Mcdonald (a pseudonym for Capt. James Dennis), Irving mentions an unusual incident:

"Early in 1932, my daughter and I were alone in the house, broad daylight, and I chanced to look through the window of the room we were in, and I saw, to my surprise, a very large cat, striped like a tiger. We ourselves did not possess a cat and I called Voirrey to come to the window to look at it. She did so, and remarked on the size of the cat, but, more especially the unusually large bull dog head it had. The cat then walked

15

away from the door of the outbuilding, where it was standing (40 to 50 feet away from us), and I then saw it was a Manx tailless cat, and I was then a little more surprised, as the pure Manx cat is usually smaller than the English. I thought this is no ordinary cat, so I slipped a cartridge into my single-barrel gun, and took "go" after him. Personally, I am very fond of cats, and do not kill for killing's sake. The cat was a little ahead of me, but easily within range, and it turned through an open gate way into a grass field. I was there a few seconds behind, and fully expected to see the cat, but no cat could be seen, look as I liked, the field was level, and there was not a bush or any roughness where he could have hidden, and the hedges were all earth, or sod hedges, as they are called here.... I detailed my experiences to my wife on her return that night, when Gef called out 'It was me you saw, Jim.' Further explanation is beyond me."

(March 4, 1935, HPC 3F 3, Harry Price archive, Senate House Library, University of London)

On another occasion, three young fishermen from the nearby city of Peel had made the trip to Doarlish Cashen, to see for themselves the "Dalby Spook." Irving invited the three men to come in and sit down. While everyone was engrossed in conversation, one of the men suddenly stopped talking and could be seen motioning with his hand, as if petting an animal. He asked Irving about their "white, pet cat" that was now sitting on his lap...despite the fact that no one else could see it. Irving explained that not only did they not have a cat, white or otherwise, but that none of his nearest neighbors owned one either.

As news about the "man-weasel" of Doarlish Cashen spread, reporters and paranormal investigators visited the farmhouse in hopes of catching a glimpse of Gef, or better yet, indulging him in lively conversation. In 1932, psychic researcher Harry Price sent his friend Capt. James Macdonald to Doarlish Cashen to see if the stories were true or not. Capt. Macdonald visited the Irving's three times between 1932 and 1935. Capt. Mcdonald never saw Gef, but heard him speak a number of times and also witnessed items such as a bottle and a china tray being thrown without any visible source.

Price, along with Richard Stanton Lambert (the founding editor of *The Listener* and an employee of the BBC and CBC), journeyed to Doarlish Cashen in July 1935, but Gef had told the Irving's beforehand that he thought Price was a "doubter" and would refuse to allow himself to be seen or heard. True to his statement, Gef "vanished" as he often liked to say and Price and Lambert were discouraged by Gefs less than welcoming demeanor.

Price and Lambert would go on to write a book about Gef (included in this book). In *"The Haunting of Cashen's Gap* (1936)," Price admits that he is perplexed by Gef. While Price makes some good points on why the case could be a hoax, he also admits that there is considerable evidence on why it could be an actual paranormal event.

Nandor Fodor Seeks a Psychological Explanation

As I was saying at the beginning of this chapter, one of the last paranormal investigators to look into the Gef phenomenon was Nandor Fodor. Fodor was one of the leading authorities on poltergeists, haunting and paranormal phenomena. At one time he was an associate of Sigmund Freud and wrote on subjects like prenatal development and dream interpretation. However, Fodor is credited mostly for his book, *"Encyclopedia of Psychic Science,"* first published in 1934.

In 1937, Fodor, who was the Research Officer for the International Institute for Psychical Research, traveled to the Isle of Man and stayed at the Irving's house for a week. By the time Fodor got involved with the mystery, Gef had been around for at least five years. Mr. Irving had written to Fodor stating that it was unlikely he would get the chance to converse with Gef, who now had become more "surly." But Fodor made the trip anyway, and, as was his habit with strangers, Gef refused to talk or make his presence known.

One night, while at the farmhouse, Fodor had rocks thrown at him. Another time the kitchen door banged twice, which the Irving's attributed to Gef. Jim Irving told Fodor that in twenty years that particular door had never banged from the wind. Despite not having much to go on, Fodor saw the case as a true mystery, since "all the probabilities are against it but all the evidence is for it."

After his visit, Fodor even wrote Gef a letter, expressing his disappointment that Gef refused to greet his guest.

"Dear Gef, I am very disappointed that you did not speak to me during the whole week which I spent here. I came from a long way and took a lot of trouble in collecting all your clever sayings … I believe you to be a very good and generous mongoose. I brought you chocolates and biscuits and I would have been happy if you had done something for me."

Initially, Fodor concluded, "I cannot prove he is an animal. I have not seen him. He did not talk to me. He claimed to be an animal. I cannot disprove that claim."

Fodor speculated that Gef was a poltergeist centered on Voirrey. However, years later he changed his mind and suggested a complex psychological theory to explain Gef based on "a split-off part" of Jim Irving's personality in order to fill his time, build his ego and feed the mental starvation from which he suffered in the wilderness of the Isle.

Voirrey Grants an Interview For FATE Magazine

Not much is known about what happened to Gef in the years after Fodor visited the Irving farm. Jim Irving passed away in 1945 from pernicious anemia. Voirrey had moved to England in 1939 to not only work as a wartime machinist, but to finally be free from the entire Gef affair. Voirrey did grant an interview in 1970 with journalist Walter McGraw which was printed in FATE magazine. Voirrey was 52, and up until that time had refused all interview requests.

McGraw spent an entire day with Voirrey and said that she was a knowledgeable conversationalist. However, she did not answer the question he most wanted answered, "What happened to Gef?"

Voirrey says she does not know. The last she remembers his being around the farm was in 1938 or 1939. He seemed to go away for longer and longer periods of time and then he just never showed up again. He had made no statements about leaving; there had been no good-byes; he simply was gone.

Gef the Talking Mongoose was covered extensively by both local newspapers and international press.

In February 1947, two years after Irving's death, the *Isle of Man Examiner* reported Leslie Graham, a retired army lieutenant who had bought Doarlish Cashen, was putting away his motorcycle one night when he was startled by an animal with gleaming eyes. It had a weasel-like appearance but it was bigger than a weasel, more like a skunk. Graham set a snare for it and in the morning found it trapped and ferocious. "It snarled and spat and clawed more venomously than anything I have ever seen." Graham clubbed it to death with a stick. The corpse was three feet long with black and yellow mottled fur. This was proof that some kind of unusual animal did once live near the Irving house.

When McGraw showed Voirrey a photo of the animal killed by Graham, she said it looked nothing like Gef. As well, Voirrey told McGraw that she hates Gef. In the early days she and Gef were inseparable, playing games and sharing sweets, but as she grew older Gef became closer to her father. Fodor noticed in 1937 and reported at that time that Gef seemed to have outstripped Voirrey in mental growth. He wrote, "Its grasp and thirst for knowledge is simply phenomenal."

By then Voirrey had found Gef and his reputation to be a burden. She was a young woman who wanted a social life and friends and more than anything else she wanted to be accepted.

"I was shy, I still am," she said. "He made me meet people I didn't want to meet. Then they said I was 'mental' or a ventriloquist. Believe me, if I was that good I would jolly well be making money from it now!

"Gef was very detrimental to my life. We were snubbed. The other children used to call me 'the spook.' I had to leave the Isle of Man and I hope that no one where I work now ever knows the story. Gef has even kept me from getting married. How could I ever tell a man's family about what happened?"

Was Gef a mongoose?

"I don't know. I know he was a small animal about nine inches to a foot long. I know he talked to us from the wainscoting. His voice was very high-pitched. He swore a lot."

The speech was not parrot-like?

"Oh, no. At first he talked to me more than anyone. We carried on regular conversations."

Was the whole Gef affair was a hoax?

"It was not a hoax and I wish it had never happened, she replied. "If my mother and I had had our way we never would have told anybody about it. But Father was sort of wrapped up in it. It was such a wonderful phenomenon that he just had to tell people about it."

After all those years, with endless questions and speculations, Voirrey summed it all up very succinctly.

"Yes, there was a little animal who talked and did all those other things. He said he was a mongoose and said we should call him Gef. I do wish he had let us alone."

Voirrey Irving passed away in 2005.

Vanished.

Voirrey with Mona.

The Winefield Chicken Murderer is Back!

By Paul Dale Roberts, HPI's Esoteric Detective

I got this phone call the other day from Josh Mayfield of Riverside. It's an interesting sighting.

Josh: Paul, I heard you will be going to Los Angeles. Do you think it is possible that you and your wife Deanna can investigate an area of Riverside while you are down here?

Paul: What for?

Josh: Well, me and my buddy saw a bunch of chickens head over to our moving car and when the chickens dispersed there was a man standing there. He looked like a man from the 1930s. As we did some research, it looks like he may be the ghost of Gordon Stewart Northcott. I saw his picture on the Internet and it was the same thing that I saw in Riverside. I am almost sure it was Gordy. What is also really strange is that I brought my dog. My dog is a German Shepherd named Mogley. Mogley started acting very strangely. Then Mogley looked at me and out from his mouth came the word Gordy. Sure there was some ruffled barks in the beginning, but the word Gordy was very clear. I couldn't believe it; my dog Mogley actually said a human word!

Paul: Wow! That is absolutely weird. I wonder if Gordy possessed your dog? By the way, what street in Riverside?

Josh: Main Street.

Paul: When did this happen?

Josh: A couple of weeks ago (talked to him on October 12th).

Paul: Did the ghost pose a threat?

Josh: No, but he looked real evil like.

Paul: How do you know what you were looking at was a ghost?

Josh: Because it vanished before me and my buddy's eyes and so did those chickens.

Paul: Who is this Gordon Stewart Northcott? Did I get the name correct?

Josh: Yes, he was known as the Wineville Chicken Murderer and he would kidnap and murder little boys. This happened in 1928. He would torture the boys on his chicken ranch. He committed all kinds of murders in Los Angeles and Riverside counties. Many people say that he used quicklime to dispose of the bodies. When the police were onto him, he fled to Canada and got nabbed in Canada. What was even more bizarre is that when I got home Mogley was acting weird again and he ran up to me and seemed like he was going to bite me. I pushed him to the side and he actually said..."you will die!"

Paul: You are telling me that your dog said "you will die!" Then it sounds like this deceased serial killer was possessing Mogley. Is Mogley back to normal again?

Josh: One particular night, Mogley jumped on my bed and he was panting, as he stood on my chest. Mogley's eyes looked like they were a bright sky blue, when in reality they are brown. I could feel Mogley's saliva drip on my chest and Mogley says in a deep human male voice..."I lust, I hate, I kill!" I screamed bloody murder and grabbed Mogley and threw him hard against the wall, he let out a loud yelp! The next day Mogley was back to normal and he seemed like he was afraid of me, because I threw him up hard against the wall. I hugged Mogley and apologized for my aggressive behavior. Since that incident I had no more problems with Mogley and he is a normal dog and no longer does he speak the English language, he speaks dog once more.

(Slight laughing).

Paul: That is one incredible story. Before you called me, my wife had a vision of a talking dog. She had this vision two days before your phone call. The dog appeared to be a German Shepherd or maybe a wolf and it was telling her to stay away, stay away. Maybe her vision is telling her to stay away from Riverside, I don't know. If you want to talk with my wife about your experience, she can conduct a blessing in your behalf and Mogley's behalf. Her name is Deanna Jaxine Stinson, and you can find her on Facebook at Sacramento Paranormal Help. Good luck Josh! Thank you for this story and if we get down to Riverside, we will look you up. Special Note: The only other talking dog I know of that is also associated with a serial killer is the Son of Sam dog. The Son of Sam supposingly received his instructions from his neighbor's dog.

Malevolent the Carmichael Talking Squirrel

Once, while at the movies with HPI paranormal investigator Sherri Ulmer, I got a phone call. My paranormal cell phone vibrated in my pocket and the number that appears was unfamiliar. I listened to my voice mail and the call is marked "urgent," so I walked out of the theatre to take the call.

Paul: Hi, I just got your call…am I hearing you right…a talking squirrel? Please explain.

Jesse: I live in Carmichael and I was not drunk or anything, but I have poltergeist activity in my house.

Paul: Poltergeist activity? And what is with the talking squirrel? Like Rocky the Squirrel? (chuckle). I couldn't hear your name clearly on the phone, what is your name again? I am sorry.

Jesse: Jesse Saldana. Please, don't laugh, I am serious. Yes, I will tell you about the squirrel, but can I talk first about the poltergeist activity first?

Paul: Sure and I apologize for laughing, I didn't mean any harm.

Jesse: That's okay, I know it sounds stupid, but it's true. Late at night, cabinets open up, chairs move across the room, knockings are heard, this all started about a year ago.

Paul: Anything significant happened a year ago?

Jesse: No, not really.

Paul: Nothing…did you purchase anything or bring anything to your home, that you would consider unusual?

Jesse: Funny you would say that, I bought some old tarot cards from an antique store.

Paul: Get rid of them! I believe that may be the cause of your problems. How much did you pay for them?

Jesse: $150.00. They were really old.

Paul: You are going to take a loss of $150.00, because you are going to get rid of them. Are you okay with that?

Jesse: Yes. How should I get rid of them?

Paul: Take them to hallowed sacred ground, like a cemetery and bury them.

Jesse: Are you sure?

Paul: Yes, I am sure, when you do that I will conduct a blessing of your home. Now tell me about the squirrel.

Jesse: Well, two nights ago there was this squirrel that was perched on my fence, I went over with my cell phone to take a picture of the squirrel and I noticed it had red eyes, it looked at me and said: "your time is near!" and it scurried off. I started crying and fell to my knees, I was so scared. Have you ever heard of anything like this?

Paul: Yes, there was a talking mongoose (actually a talking weasel) named Gef and in the 1930s he was talking to all of the villagers on the Isle of Man. Gef claimed he was born in New Delhi, India in 1852. He was full of wit and sometimes threatening remarks. He was even known to sing Home on the Range. Some people theorize Gef was possessed by an evil spirit. Have you seen this squirrel again?

Jesse: No, should I be afraid?

Paul: Extremely! This squirrel is definitely malevolent and is connected to the poltergeist activity. I want you to get rid of the tarot cards immediately and I want you to bury them at: -------------- Cemetery. Will you do this?

Jesse: Yes, tomorrow.

Paul: Okay, keep me appraised on what occurs after the burial. If the activity continues, I will schedule you for an investigation and cleansing. When you get rid of the cards, I will come over for a blessing of your home, are you okay with that?

Jesse: Yes! Thank you for all your help! I will be in touch.

Paul: You are welcome and god bless.

· · · · ·

Halo Paranormal Investigations – HPI International.

www.cryptic916.com/

jazmaonline.boards.net/

www.facebook.com/#!/groups/HPIinternational/

Sacramento Haunted Paranormal Hotline: (916) 203-7503 – 4 Advice & Investigations

Email: azmaonline@gmail.com

A ſtraunge.

and terrible Wunder wrought
very late in the pariſh Church
of Bongay: a Towvn of no great di-
ſtance from the citie of Norwich, namely the fourth of this Auguſt, in ý yeare of
our Lord 1577. in a great tempeſt of violent raine, lightning, and thunder, the
like whereof hath been ſel-
dome ſeene.

With the appearance of an horrible ſha-
ped thing, ſenſibly perceived of the
people then and there
aſſembled.

Drawen into a plain method according to the written copye.
by Abraham Fleming.

31

The Squonk (An Excerpt)
By Hercules Invictus

According to the lore of long-ago loggers, the Squonk always manifested as a small loose-skinned entity covered with unattractive warts and moles. It is difficult to ascertain much about the Squonk's form beyond this. It has been referred to as a bird with lips and teeth. Artists have depicted it as a humanoid, a hound, and a rat-like biped.

The Squonk was seemingly cursed with enough self-consciousness to realize how wretched it must have appeared to humans. An odd concern for a monstrous intelligence, unless — like the gorgon Medusa — it was once human. It is said that though the Squonk's lament was often heard, the creature itself was seldom seen.

Tracking the Squonk was a task best left for bright, moon-lit nights or during periods of frost. The creature's trail of tears glistened eerily at such times and, if followed, would lead you to its well-hidden lair. If you hoped to catch a glimpse of one you had to respond to its heart-rending lament by expressing the depths of your very own private sorrow. The Squonk would be curious to discover what monstrosity could possibly be more wretched than itself.

In the dawn of the 20th century a hunter, J.P. Wentling (Wentley by some accounts), is said to have actually captured a

Squonk. He followed the sad trail of shiny tears, waited patiently to hear the unearthly weeping, responded in kind and when the entity eventually manifested he quickly nabbed it in a sack. It struggled and sobbed for a while, then abruptly ceased. The sack grew lighter. When the hunter opened it he found that naught remained of his catch but a layer of frothy slime.

By 1915 the wild hemlock forests of northern Pennsylvania had been tamed and humbled. The Squonk's natural habitat was no more. Occasionally one was sighted in the region's hardwood forests, but the creature seemed fated to fade into folklore, to survive in memory as a curious entry in fringe books on vanishing local lore.

© Hercules Invictus

The Squonk, as portrayed on the Genesis album cover "A Trick of the Tail,"
has a decidedly "Gef-like" appearance.

WHEN THE POLTERGEIST FINDS ITS VOICE

By Tim R. Swartz

It can be terrifying enough when a poltergeist makes its appearance in a household. Rocks thrown about, strange bangs on the walls, moving furniture, items disappearing and then reappearing, this is enough to set anyone on edge. However, when a poltergeist finds its voice and starts to talk, you know that events have decidedly taken a turn for the worse.

It is still debated whether Gef was a poltergeist, or something else. Unlike traditional "talking poltergeists" which usually takes time before they start vocalizing, Gef started talking right away. He then followed up with other poltergeist types of tricks (throwing things, moving and hiding household items, knocks-raps and bangs etc.).

Poltergeist activity has been recorded throughout history and is probably the most prolific of all supernatural events. One of the earliest accounts was from around 500 C.E. when St. Germain, Bishop of Auxerre, was bothered by a spirit that battered the walls of a shelter the Bishop was spending the night in with showers of rocks. Another early case was the Bingen poltergeist, which comes from the **Annales Fuldenses** or **Annals of Fulda**. This incident happened near Bingen in present-day Bavaria around 856-858 C.E. A farmer was plagued by a stone-throwing ghost who shook the walls of his house "as though the men of the place were striking it with hammers," set crops on fire and also shouted obscenities and accusations at the farmer suggesting that he had slept with the daughter of his foremen. The poltergeist would follow the man around and fearful neighbors would refuse to allow him near their homes.

The Bishop of Mainz sent priests with holy relics who attested to hearing the poltergeist denouncing the farmer for adultery. When the priests sang hymns and sprinkled holy water, the poltergeist threw stones and cursed at them.

The Bingen poltergeist had many typical features of a poltergeist that are still repeated in modern times. The fact that this poltergeist could talk is something that has been seen in other cases, but nevertheless, it really doesn't happen that often.

Is A Poltergeist A Ghost?

Poltergeist phenomenon is often placed in the same niche as ghosts and hauntings. The implication is that a poltergeist is a ghost, i.e. a human that has died and returned in spirit form. There is no doubt that there are similarities between ghosts and poltergeist activity. However, a ghostly haunting often tends to have the visual element; for example, a glowing figure dressed in old fashioned clothes is seen walking down a hallway. A haunting also repeats in the same way on a regular basis, much like a recording that is played back over and over. In long-term ghostly hauntings, a ghost will usually ignore entreaties from the living and shows no sign of awareness of its surroundings.

The Devil and the Drum, from the frontispiece to the third edition of "Saducismus Triumphatus" (1700). The illustration depicts "The Drummer of Tedworth," an early report of poltergeist activity that erupted in the John Mompesson household. The disturbances continued for months where the children's bedsteads would shake and levitate into the air and objects were thrown violently around the room.

Below: Not much has changed. Poltergeist activity has remained consistent for centuries. From objects being thrown by unseen hands to weird knocks and raps on the wall, the poltergeist relies on the same types of tricks.

Poltergeist activity, instead, operates in a completely different fashion. A poltergeist almost never makes an "appearance" and becomes visible, but as with ghostly hauntings, there are always exceptions. A poltergeist can do things such as move heavy furniture, instantaneously teleport objects, produce explosive sounds and disgusting odors, create rain inside a building, cause spontaneous fires and other things that seem to be outside of our current understanding of physics.

A poltergeist is extremely aware of its surroundings, and will often quickly respond to suggestions by observers and other external stimuli. This shows that there is some kind of "intelligence" behind its pranks and not just some random psychokinesis (PK). This intelligence, along with an ability to communicate, will manifest in a myriad of ways. Pieces of paper with strange messages appear; writing on the walls, children's toys will be arranged to make words, and, perhaps the most shocking, they will sometimes start to speak out loud.

When a poltergeist achieves speech, it generally starts out as animal-like growls and whispers that slowly evolve into discernible words. Most poltergeists never reach this stage of their development, but once they do, a clear "personality" emerges from what were previously just random events.

L'Antidemon de Mascon

One early case of a talking poltergeist happened in Mâcon, France in 1612 when a Calvinist pastor named Francois Perreaud, (or Perrault), became the target of a very unsettling poltergeist. Perreaud's poltergeist made its first appearance on September 19, 1612 when invisible hands started shaking bed curtains and tossing bed clothes onto the floor. This continued for several nights and then escalated when Perreaud and his family heard "A frightful din in the kitchen consisting of unearthly rumblings and knockings, accompanied by the sounds of plates, pots, and pans being hurled against the walls." Perreaud rushed to the kitchen, expecting to find his kitchen destroyed, but was shocked to find that everything was normal and the kitchenware was in its place.

Eventually a voice that was "very distinct and understandable, although somewhat husky" was heard in the house. It sang, "Twenty-two pennies, twenty-two pennies," then repeated the word, "Minister" several times. Perreaud said to the voice, "Get thee behind me, Satan, the Lord commands you."

The voice kept saying "Minister, minister," until the exasperated Perreaud snapped, "Yes, I am indeed a minister and a servant of the living God before whose majesty you tremble."

"I am not saying otherwise," the voice replied.

Once the poltergeist began speaking, it proved to be difficult to shut it up. It recited the Ten Commandments, followed by the Our Father, the Apostles' Creed, and other prayers. It also sang Psalms and recited accurate personal details about Perreaud's family. The voice claimed that it was from the Pays de Vaud, which was at that time infamous for its witch hunts.

The voice told wild stories, made inappropriate jokes and often acted like a child and teased the maid. It was also able to expertly mimic the voices of various Mâcon residents. It also took on several different identities. At one time the voice claimed to be the valet of the original entity, who had left the house and was now in Chambery.

On November 25, the voice announced that it would no longer speak, but its antics in the form of throwing stones, tying knots in the mane and tail of Perreaud's horse, and other typical poltergeist stunts, continued through until December when it finally disappeared forever.

Different Personalities, Different Voices

The Bell Witch poltergeist in 1817 was very similar to the Mâcon poltergeist due to the fact that "the witch" was extremely talkative and could imitate the voices of people from the area. The poltergeist was said to speak at a nerve-racking pitch when displeased, while at other times it sang and talked in low musical tones. In one instance, it was alleged to have repeated, verbatim, sermons administered by two preachers, occurring at separate locations, that took place simultaneously. The sermons recited by the witch were verified by people attending the churches as being identical in voice, tone, inflection, and content. The poltergeist was even known to attend church and sing along with the congregation, using the most beautiful voice anyone had ever heard.

As well, the poltergeist had the ability to change personalities in the middle of conversations with the Bells' or their visitors. The witch had five distinct personalities, each with different voices and traits which made it easy for the family to separate the perpetrator of the moment. These voices were named "Black dog," "Mathematics," "Cypocryphy" and "Jerusalem."

This ability to produce "different personalities" also shows up in other poltergeist cases, creating a belief that there are a number of different entities haunting a house.

The Bell Witch was very fond of talking about religion and philosophy for hours on end, especially with John Bell Jr. The witch had developed a respect John Bell Jr. due to his tendency to stand up to its abusive behavior. In 1828, the poltergeist reappeared to John Bell Jr. telling him, "John, I am in hopes you will not be as angry at me on this visit as you were on my last. I shall do nothing to cause you offense; I have been in the West Indies for seven years."

Despite his misgivings, the poltergeist had long talks with him about the past, the present and the future. Years later, he told his son, Dr. Joel Thomas Bell, the details of the poltergeist's discussions. A book was published in 1934, *The Bell Witch - A Mysterious Spirit*, which supposedly was met by outrage by other members of the Bell family who felt that details of "the family problem" should not have been made public.

For a more complete history of the Bell Witch poltergeist, see *The Bell Witch Project* by Timothy Green Beckley, published by Inner Light-Global Communications.

The Shawville Poltergeist

When a poltergeist does find its voice it seems to take great delight in spinning wild tales of its identity and origin. It may at one time say it is the ghost of someone who died years before, only to change its tune later and profess to be the devil or a demon. Like the Bell Witch, the Shawville poltergeist (also known as the Dagg poltergeist), enjoyed entertaining visitors by telling obscene stories and conversely, singing hymns in an "angelic voice."

The Shawville Poltergeist took place in the Ottawa Valley, Quebec in 1889 and centered on the farm and family of George

Dagg. The incidents started with what appeared to be animal feces streaked along the farmhouse floor. At first, a young farmhand named Dean was blamed since he was known to come into the house with dirty shoes. Nevertheless, after the boy had been fired, the strange incidents continued with crockery moving, fires starting spontaneously and windows being smashed.

The Dagg family's eleven-year-old adopted daughter, Dina-Burden McLean, was also physically attacked by the entity when it pulled her hair so hard that her braid was almost torn off. Later, when Dina's grandmother was making up one of the bedrooms, the girl shouted, "Oh grandmother, see the big, black thing pulling off the bed clothes!" The woman could see the sheets being pulled up, but couldn't see what was doing it. She handed Dina a whip, telling the girl to strike out at the invisible being. Dinah struck the air a few times and both the girl and her grandmother heard a sound like a pig squealing.

A few days later a piece of paper bearing the message "You gave me fifteen cuts" was found nailed to the wall.

After this incident Dina claimed that she was hearing a strange, gruff voice that followed her around saying bad words to her. Soon, the entire family and others could hear the gruff, man's voice who identified itself "as the Devil." Not everyone was convinced the voice was a supernatural being and blamed Dina for everything. At one point her mouth was filled with water, yet the voice could still be clearly heard by everyone in the room.

Much like the Bell witch, the Shawville poltergeist enjoyed the attention and would talk for hours. It would often give conflicting stories on what it was. Previously it said it was the devil, later, it claimed to be the spirit of an old man who had died 20 years earlier. When George asked it why it was bothering his family, it replied, "Just for fun."

It also admitted setting small fires in the house, but again only for its amusement. "I set the fires in the daytime, when you could see them. I like fires, but I didn't want to burn the house down."

After several months of activity, the voice announced that it was going away. When word got out, crowds began gathering at the house to witness the event. The voice was happy to answer questions from the crowd, but now it claimed, "I am an angel from Heaven, sent by God to drive away that fellow."

"You don't believe that I am an angel because my voice is coarse," it said to the crowd. "I will show you I don't lie, but always tell the truth." Instantly its voice took on an "incredible sweetness," and it started singing a hymn:

"I am waiting, I am waiting, to call you dear sinner, Come to the savior, come to him now, won't you receive Him right now, right now, Oh! List, now he is calling today, He is calling you to Jesus, move! Come to Him now, Come to Him, dear brothers and sisters, Come to Him now."

Witness testimony agreed that the poltergeist sang with such a beautiful voice that many of the women were reduced to tears. After several hours of singing, the poltergeist said goodbye, saying it would return the next morning and show itself to Dinah and the other children.

The next morning the children breathlessly told their parents that "a beautiful man, he took little Johnny and me in his arms... he went to Heaven and was all red."

Under questioning, the children described a man dressed in white with a lovely face with long white hair. He also had ribbons and "pretty things" all over his clothes and a gold object with stars on his head. The man reached down and picked them up saying that they were fine children.

Dinah said he had spoken to her as well, telling her that everyone thought he was not an angel, but he would show he was. Then he had "gone up to Heaven." Questioned further, she said he seemed to rise up in the air and disappear in a kind of fire that blazed from his feet.

The Shawville poltergeist was almost forgotten until 1957 when 64-year-old Thomas Dagg, who was born after the events, confirmed that his parents and older siblings were convinced that everything that had happened to them was true and not a hoax. Thomas told reporters that he was sure that the uncanny episode "was the work of the Devil."

Compared to other poltergeist events, talking poltergeists seem to be in a category all by themselves. They may start out the same, annoying pranks, strange noises, showers of rocks and other debris, but then they seem to turn a corner and gain energy to a point where a consciousness and personality emerges. The personality is much like a child or mentally challenged adult, but it is a personality nevertheless.

Both the Bell Witch and the Shawville poltergeist exhibit almost identical personality traits. Both were fond of using obscene language and taking on the roles of different characters. Both entities were never shy about talking for hours in front of multiple witnesses. In fact, they seemed to thrive on the attention. They also claimed the ability to travel instantaneously to far off locations, bringing back information that could be verified later.

Gef The Talking Mongoose

The central focus of this book deals with Gef the talking Mongoose. His case is so unique in paranormal history that despite the upfront absurdity of it all—a mongoose apparently as intelligent and talking like a human—researchers are still writing and debating the story almost 90 years later.

The similarities between Gef and other talking poltergeists cannot be ignored. Most that has been written about Gef attest to his shyness and amazing abilities throw and move things right at the moment when no one was looking (a very distinctive poltergeist trait.) As well, it has been said that no one other than the Irving's ever saw Gef, or even heard him speak for any length of time.

Charles Morrison, a lifelong friend of Jim Irving, heard Gef speak on two occasions, and was convinced it was no hoax. In his "Amplified Statement" to Harry Price, Morrison described hearing a loud, clear voice from behind the boards in the kitchen.

"Tell Arthur (Morrison's son) not to come...He doesn't believe. I won't speak if he does come; I'll blow his brains out with a 3d cartridge." Together with "heavy thumping on the ceiling and behind the boards in the kitchen as much as a strong man could do." Morrison was impressed by the noises quickly occurring from all over the house.

Morrison also noted: "...at 3pm, came a voice from the porch, 'Charlie.' Very loud and clear...At 3.5 a voice: 'Is Arthur coming?' this in the kitchen. A screech and then a loud thump the other end of the house!" (C. Morrison: Report by Mr CA Morrison, 1935, SHL, HPC 3F 6.)

Charles son, Arthur Morrison, was at first was skeptical of the whole Gef affair. However, he changed his mind when he visited the Irving's on March 7, 1932.

"On my arrival at Mr Irving's farmhouse a screeching voice said, 'Hullo Arthur.' To which I replied, 'Hullo.' It then said, 'Call me Gef. I am an earth bound spirit. Before I saw you I was going to blow your brains out with a 3d cartridge, but I like you now.' Quietness for a few minutes, then loud knockings on the walls in various parts of the house. Suddenly it said, 'Vanished.' All this happened between 5pm and 6pm. At about 8 o'clock, Gef reappeared. 'I'm going to keep you awake all tonight.' 'You are not going to keep your promise, I hope. What have I done to deserve it?' I asked. 'You are a doubter.' In the vicinity of 9 o'clock, while dozing in bed, I heard something moving about underneath and thought it a rat or mouse. Peering underneath the bed, I perceived a pair of piercing eyes. They seemed smaller than a cat's eyes look like in the dark. An uncanny voice said, 'Now do you believe? Don't you dare to upset Jimo with any sceptical remarks' at the same time making a spitting noise. Jimo referred to Mr Irving. All that night I was kept awake at intervals by animal noises. The next morning I apologised to Mr Irving for previously disbelieving in the stories of extraordinary manifestations taking place. I positively had all the Irving family at home at the time under observation. There was absolutely no fraud of any description." (A. Morrison: Letter to Nandor Fodor, 23 Feb 1937, SPR research archive, Cambridge Univ. Library, "Talking Mongoose" file.)

Even though it can't be proven, Voirrey was probably essential for Gefs existence. Somehow she provided the energy for Gef to either exist, or, if Gef was something along the lines of an elemental – or even an ancient "artificial intelligence" (discussed at the end of this chapter), it was awakened and sustained chiefly by Voirrey.

Skeptics insist that Voirrey was using ventriloquism to produce Gef's voice…something that she always denied. However, another poltergeist case that happened years later may offer an explanation on how Gef may have been able to talk.

The Enfield Poltergeist

In 1977, a house in the north London suburb of Enfield was the scene of violent disturbances of apparently paranormal origin. Peggy Hodgson and her four children, Margaret, Janet, John and Billy found themselves besieged with frightening activity such as heavy furniture being moved, toys flying around the house of their own volition, eleven-year-old Janet levitated and deposited in different places at different times, and even more disturbing, a strange voice that seemed to come from Janet and sometimes Margaret.

In December 1977, three months after the start of the disturbances, a gruff voice began to emanate from Janet. It started as a series of whistles and dog-like barks, and developed into a voice that sounded nothing like Janet's. The voice said it was "Bill Wilkins" and claimed that he had lived in the house (the previous occupant was in fact a Bill Wilkins who had died in the house, a fact apparently unknown to Janet). The voice swore and used foul language that was not typical of the girl. Janet said that when the voice spoke, she felt something like a hand on the back of her neck.

However, Bill wasn't the only alleged spirit who made contact. In total around ten voices came through that identified themsleves as Joe Watson, Fred, Dirty Dick, Andrew Gardner and Stuart Certain.

To eliminate the possibility that Janet was faking the voice, her mouth was taped shut, which did not stop the voice. As well, another time her mouth was filled with water and the voice continued to be heard, albeit somewhat subdued. In early January 1978, Margaret started to speak in a similar voice, but without the same intensity or duration as Janet's.

During the investigations, recordings of the voice were made. A contact microphone placed on the back of Janet's head picked up what appeared to be a different and louder sound than her normal voice. An experiment using a laryngograph conducted by John Hasted, a physicist at London's Birbeck College, along with Adrian Fourcin, a phonetics expert at University College, London, showed an effect known as plica ventricularis. Janet and Margaret were producing sounds using muscle tension in their throat which can produce sounds independent of the vocal chords. The only problem was that using this method is extremely damaging to the throat, resulting in weeks of hoarseness and a sore throat, neither of which was exhibited by the girls who could produce the voice for several hours at a time.

Could this have been the same method that Gef used to produce his voice from Voirrey? But instead of a low, gruff, male voice, Gef's voice was high-pitched to a point that it seemed impossible to have been produced by a human. It could be that whatever intelligence is responsible for these kinds of paranormal activities are dependent not only on their human hosts, but the location may also play a significant role. Once Voirrey grew older and tired of Gef's antics, Gef grew more sullen and disappeared for longer periods of time. Once Voirrey moved away to England, Gef vanished once and for all. However, Voirrey's older sister, Elsie, said that on the day that Jim Irving passed away, there were strange noises heard in the house and a small broom on the mantle moved around by itself. The essence of Gef may still have been around the farmhouse, but without a proper source of power (Voirrey) it could no longer produce an independent personality.

Like Voirrey, Janet Hodgson said in the documentary "Interview with a Poltergesit" in 2007: "I know from my own experience that it was real. It lived off me, off my energy. Call me mad or a prankster if you like. Those events did happen. The poltergeist was with me—and I feel in a sense that he always will be."

The Voice From The Stove

In the same time period that Gef was active, another talking poltergeist appeared in Zaragoza, Spain. The Palazon family was living in an apartment complex on Gascón Gotor street when in September, 1934 they started to hear maniacal laughter and voices coming from inside their home. At first the voice sounded like a woman, but later it would change and appear to be a man speaking. The family was perplexed by the strange sounds, but kept it to themselves for fear of ridicule.

When the din coming from the apartment became too much, neighbors called the police. The voice then started shouting: "Cowards, cowards. You called the police. Cowards!"

When they arrived, the households young maid, named Pascuala Alcocer, told police that when she was trying to light the wood stove, she heard a loud voice coming from the stove, or its chimney, saying, "You're hurting me!"

The police checked the apartment but couldn't find any source for the mysterious voice. Word quickly spread and hundreds of people gathered outside of Building #2 in hopes of hearing the "duende" (goblin) for themselves.

Local police and judges personally investigated the home, forcing the family to move out as they shut off electricity and phone service as they tore the place apart. This enraged the voice and it shouted to everyone that it would kill them and all the residents in the building.

Authorities also brought in psychiatrists to question Pascuala, whom they suspected of hoaxing everything. The doctors suggested that Pascuala was mentally ill and that she was producing the voice through subconscious ventriloquism. At one point they sent the maid on a vacation along with the family, yet the voice continued to speak. Even moving every resident out of Building #2 failed to stop it.

Whatever the source, the voice was able to see what was going on around the building. It would guess the number of people that were in a room at a time, it would interact with police officers directly when they asked it what it wanted.

"Do you want money?"

"No!"

"Do you want a job?"

Pascuala Alcocer shows the chimney where the voice of the "Duende" seemed to emanate. The Duende of Zaragoza, Spain occurred around the same time as Gef.

Below: Poltergeist phenomena surrounding Janet and Margaret Hodgson eventually started producing strange voices claiming to be discarnate spirits. This could be similar to how the voice of Gef came from Voirrey Irving.

Above: The Dagg home as it looks now. The Shawville poltergeist also known as the Dagg poltergeist is a historical, and well documented case in Canada.

Below: The home of John Bell and his family. The focal point for the Bell Witch haunting.

"No!"

"Every man wants something."

"I'm not a man!"

One of the original builders was brought in to take measurements of the kitchen, but the voice interrupted saying: "Don't worry, it measures 75 centimeters." The mason was so scared he left the building never to come back leaving his tools behind in a closet.

Eventually the voice vanished just as mysteriously as it arrived. Pascuala Alcocer, much like Voirrey Irving, went into seclusion lamenting up until her death years later that "the voice from the wall ruined her life."

The Poltergeist As An Elemental

There are many more cases of talking poltergeists that have been carefully researched and chronicled, and probably hundreds more that were never reported for fear of ridicule. The poltergeist by itself is an oddity in the world of paranormal research, and the talking poltergeist goes even further as a head-scratcher due to its outright off-the-wall high strangeness.

All kinds of theories on the true nature of the poltergeist have been suggested. Black magic and curses as the cause of poltergeists are popular in countries such as Brazil where spiritism is still practiced. Folk lore concerning elemental spirits such as fairies, hobs and goblins show that they were also fond of mischievous tricks such as throwing rocks, starting fires and stealing household objects.

55

Middle Eastern folklore and Muslim theology concerning the djinn and their amazing powers also have similarities to the poltergeist. The djinn are beings with free will that once lived on Earth but were sent away by God to a world parallel to mankind. The word djinn comes from an Arabic root meaning "hidden from sight," so they are physically invisible from man as their description suggests.

The djinn will take possession of buildings or locations and torment any person who goes to live there. They throw rocks at people. They can levitate and cause objects to disappear. A djinn can quickly travel great distances. One of the powers of the djinn, is that they are able to take on any physical form they like. Thus, they can appear as humans, animals and anything else. They can mimic the voices of deceased humans, claiming to be spirits or Satan. They enjoy playing tricks and frightening people. In fact, they can feel strong emotions such as fear or grief and gain energy from these strong emotions.

Like humans, the djinn have distinct personalities. There are those who are of low intelligence, quick to anger and are fond of playing tricks. Others have a superior intellect and act more along the lines of guardian angels rather than tricksters.

It is interesting to consider that the poltergeist could be an elemental spirit rather than a human. This could explain why poltergeists (especially the more energetic talking poltergeist) are resistant and very hostile, to attempts to get rid of them by using religious methods. If a poltergeist is not a human spirit or a demon in a Christian, Jewish or Muslim tradition, attempts to use exorcism are pretty much useless.

Could The Poltergeist Be An Artificial Intelligence?

Considering that the poltergeist could be something other than a human spirit, the website *The State of Reality*, (www.thestateofreality.com) states to be "the combined effort of four professional remote viewers that have set out to share their project findings regarding socially significant, anomalous target sets." On this site there is an interesting article concerning their remote viewing of the Bell Witch incident.

Jeff Coley writes that the team's result of their remote viewing attempt came up with the concept of "Something contained, or restrained inside an enclosure. Often this container was sketched and described to be like a bottle, while at other times as a box of some kind, which acted as an enclosure or a tomb. One viewer's session described this object as an ossuary, similar to what a collector of antique relics might possess within their private collection. Other sessions described what looked suspiciously similar to the idea of a Genie bottle."

According to Coley something had been contained inside a bottle or box. The viewers described it as a phantom, and intelligence and a thought form. The remote viewing work describes the purpose of this thing as having to do with amusement, recreation, performance, and the idea of sending a message. The viewers also described that the phenomenon was associated with something destructive in nature. One viewer notes that it is like a parasite or a time-bomb that somehow escaped or was accidently released.

The opinion by the remote viewers was that whatever the Bell Witch was, it had been deliberately contained as a punishment eons ago. Three of the viewers described guards who seem to be keeping this thing bottled-up. One viewer described these guards as ethereal, floating, muscular "brutes," almost like otherworldly prison guards, while another viewer described something like a sentry, guarding and patrolling.

It almost sounds like the Bell Witch (and it even admitted to John Bell Jr. that it was millions of years old) was an artificial intelligence that had been created by a highly advanced and now vanished civilization that could have been terrestrial or even extraterrestrial. Its purpose might have been to entertain and teach but somehow became uncontrollable and had to be contained.

This is just speculation of course. But considering how unusual and powerful talking poltergeists can be, is it really so far-fetched to say that these invisible intelligences might be a form of artificial intelligence? Not an intelligence contained within a machine, but an artificial intelligence without a physical form…in other words, an artificial "spirit."

Perhaps these AI's were locked away millions of years ago for some reason. As time wore on, some have managed to escape their confinement and then proceed to wreak havoc in the area where they were kept. Perhaps they have limited energy that can no longer be "recharged." This could explain why they disappear so abruptly and completely, never to be heard from again.

This could also be a factor concerning Gef. Doarlish Cashen was said to have been built sometime in the early 19th century. The way it was constructed, as well as its size when compared to other, more modest farmhouses in the region, suggests a possible medieval origin. The area around Doarlish Cashen was obviously occupied much earlier than that even. Less than three hundred yards southeast of the house is a mound, that is presumed to be prehistoric; about five hundred yards northwest are the remains of a cairn circle and a cairn grave, dated to the Bronze Age. Just over half a mile southwest is a tumulus, near to the Sound Road, there being other tumuli and cairns situated along this ancient path.

Local folklore also suggests that Doarlish Cashen had previously been the setting for weird phenomena. Years before the Irving's had settled on the island, some men that were digging near the farmhouse, unearthed a flat stone covering a funerary urn which contained black ashes. They quickly buried it in the hedge-bank.

Years later, a young man hunting rabbits thought he saw a rabbit bolting into the same hedge that the urn had been buried. He began pulling away the stones and soil, and while doing so he felt something invisible pushing him back. When this happened a second time, a sudden fear took him and he ran down the hillside till he reached his home.

The belief in Fairies or Elves (also known as "Ferish") was once prevalent in the Isle of Man, and had not altogether died out in the 1930s. Manx folklore concerning Fairies held that whenever baking and churning was taking place in a household, a small bit of dough and butter was stuck on the wall or on a shelf for the Fairies consumption. It should be noted that biscuits and butter were a favorite snack for Gef.

The earliest inhabitants of Man believed that there were magicians, enchanters, and enchantresses that lived on the island. They had spirits at their command, and were proficient in the occult sciences. It was thought that those who practiced witchcraft were able to create an imp or familiar spirit that was available to do whatever it was directed. By the aid of this imp, the witch was able to travel, unseen, throughout the island, and transform herself into various shapes, particularly those of cats and hares.

When you look at past cases of talking poltergeists, they display personalities that if they were human subjects, doctors would describe them as psychotic or schizophrenic. If my thesis is correct, this madness could be the result of millions of years of lonely confinement, with little hope of rescue. The human mind would self-destruct in a matter of months. Consider what this amount of time could have done to an artificial mind.

Rather than fear and loathe these tortured entities, a better solution would be to offer them kindness and understanding. For any creature with a soul, even if it is an artificial soul, deserves happiness and even love. This is a difficult concept considering the torture these things have brought upon their victims, but even a savage dog will eventually respond to a kind heart.

Could the poltergeist respond as well?

THE
HAUNTING
OF
CASHEN'S
GAP

A MODERN 'MIRACLE' INVESTIGATED

HARRY PRICE & R. S. LAMBERT

**The Haunting of Cashen's Gap – A Modern "Miracle"
Investigated by Harry Price and R.S. Lambert**

First published in 1936

CONTENTS

1. DRAWING BY GEORGE SCOTT OF GEF FROM PARTICULARS SUPPLIED BY MR. IRVING AND THE 'MONGOOSE' HIMSELF

2. PHOTOGRAPH OF A GREY MONGOOSE AT THE ZOOLOGICAL GARDENS

INTRODUCTION

THE following pages are an essay in the Veracious but Unaccountable. Whether looked at from the point of view of psychology, of psychical research, of anthropology, or of sociology, this true story of Gef is very odd. We have been moved to set it down in as full a form as possible in order that every one interested – including, we hope, posterity – may be in a position to form their own judgment about it.

To believers it will represent a proof of miracle; to skeptics a lesson in the laws of evidence. Some will call it nonsense from first to last; others will admit it to be at least, as good as most ghost stories. Throughout we have sought to avoid mere credulity on the one hand and prejudiced skepticism on the other. There may be readers who will be disappointed that we have at the end no cut-and-dried solution of the mystery to offer; but this only suggests that the facts, as we have honestly tried to set them forth, are susceptible of various explanations.

For obvious reasons we have had to alter the names of some of our witnesses; but the originals of their testimony, together with a complete set of the correspondence with Mr. Irving, and the objects which constitute the visual evidence for Gef, are all filed for reference at the offices of the University of London Council for Psychical Investigation, 13D Roland Gardens, South Kensington, S.W.7. We have to thank Mr. James T. Irving for the assistance which he gave us, particularly in the earlier stages of our inquiry. We have also to thank Captain MacDonald for putting at our disposal the reports of his several visits to Doarlish Cashen; and Mr. Northwood for coming forward and subjecting himself to cross-examination on the record of his own strange experiences.

November 15th 1935

Harry Price, R.S. Lambert

CHAPTER 1

DOARLISH CASHEN: THE BACKGROUND
OF THE MYSTERY

ON the shoulder of a windswept down, seven hundred and twenty-five feet above sea-level on the west coast of the Isle of Man, stands one of the loneliest farmsteads in Britain – Doarlish Cashen, or Cashen's Gap, as it may be rendered out of the Manx. To reach it you must come right away from the tourist-ridden resorts which provide Lancashire with her summer playground. Man is an isle of contrasts.

Out of busy Douglas - a miniature Blackpool - it is but a few minutes' drive into quiet lanes and pretty valleys, where petrol-pumps, advertisements, and road-houses are surprisingly scarce, and even large estates and other signs of wealth and luxury are absent. It is a country of small farms and cottages, resembling Cornwall but less rugged and more varied, or South Wales without industrialism.

Outside the tourist resorts a hard and scanty living has to be wrung from a none-too-favourable soil. And in winter the island, though spared severe frosts, is windswept from the north-west to a degree which makes trees rare and restricts vegetation largely to sheltered spots where, however, semi-tropical plants such as palms manage to flourish.

On all sides but the north the island is edged with high cliffs or grassy downs, indented with ravines or glens, down which shunt streams rush to the sea. These glens are the beauty-spots of Man; and one of the choicest of them, Glen Maye, two miles from the old capital of Man, Peel, is the starting-point for reaching Doarlish Cashen.

A few whitewashed cottages and an inn cluster above the waterfall which marks the entrance to the Glen-a rocky chasm choked with a profuse vegetation of ferns, trees, and flowering shrubs which almost shut out the sunlight and hide the path which winds down by the bank of the stream towards the sea-shore.

Formerly Glen Maye was haunted by a water-sprite – indeed, the whole romantic neighbourhood is one where superstition dies hard. 'Wise women' (the Manx term for witches) may be all but extinct, but their stock- in-trade-spells and charms, particularly against certain illnesses - still enjoy profitable currency.

At the head of the Glen, beyond the village post office, a stony path parts from the road and winds up among the hills. Soon there are no more trees, and the track is sheltered only by sod hedges; in summer these are clad in a profusion of wild flowers-drifts of harebells (bluebells), and clusters of scarlet fuchsias-but in winter they are bare and forlorn, accentuating the bleak and monotonous appearance of the landscape.

At intervals the track skirts the ruins of cottages and farmsteads, which testify to the depopulation of the district in recent years. Arable farming upon a mere four inches of soil has long been unprofitable here; the land has fallen back to rough grass, and now pastures no more than a few sheep.

At last, after about an hour of scrambling ascent, the path turns a fold in the downs and terminates, rather suddenly, before

Doarlish Cashen. The farmstead, perched upon a treeless, shrub less slope, seems utterly isolated from the world. No cart can reach it; no other farm is visible from it; and its nearest neighbour lies a mile away. On the other hand, on a clear day what a natural panorama unfolds before it!

Mile upon mile of heathered down falls away to the sea, which is ever changing its colour, its horizon, and the degree of its apparent steepness. To the south, the eye follows a succession of promontories and islands; to the west it catches glimpses, across St. Patrick's Channel, of the shadowy coast of Ireland, the Mountains of Mourne. At midsummer Doarlish Cashen seems to lie out upon the roof of the world, basking in sunshine; but at midwinter it shrinks within itself, shivering under the lash of continual wind and ram.

Approaching the farm, you come upon a house with three outbuildings roofed with corrugated iron, roughly grouped about a grassy 'yard.' This house, which faces west: presents a grey and melancholy appearance, being built of slate slabs joined with concrete and faced with cement. Its concrete foundation is much cracked, and its walls are streaked with crevices caulked with pitch. A small, projecting porch shelters from the gales the front door, which opens towards the south.

Immediately upon entering the house the visitor is struck by its somber interior. Not only are the windows few and small, and mostly not made to open; the whole of the interior is paneled with match-boarding, which has been stained a deep dark brown, almost verging upon black. Beams, ceilings, and walls, all of them absorb the light, and impose a mysterious darkness upon the rooms. The ceilings too are low, not much above seven feet and six inches in height; while awkward steps and projecting lintels of doors and stairhead make movement indoors slow for the stranger.

Entering through the porch, the visitor finds himself facing a short and irregular staircase, carpeted but without rods, leading to the upper floor; to the left of this staircase is a tiny parlour, about eight feet square; to the right extends the principal living-room of the house, about twelve feet by ten in size.

At the far, or east, end of this room is a door opening (beneath the stairs) into a narrow pantry kitchen which occupies the back of the house behind the parlour. Both the neat parlour and the larger living- room are more comfortably and tastefully furnished than one might expect to find in such an out-of-the-way place.

On the walls hang pictures of a Maori chief with tattooed face, two large water-colours of street scenes in Istanbul, and a water-colour of a group of horses and dogs reputed to be by Landseer. The furniture includes a cushioned sofa, five or six chairs, and a table large enough to seat an equivalent number of people.

The fire-place with kitchen range occupies the centre of the south wall; in a recess to the right is kept a gramophone, with a few records; and in a corresponding, partly cup-boarded recess to the left some books and papers upon a shelf. On a sideboard against the east wall stand one or two pieces of plate, including a christening-cup in Sheffield silver-plate, at night the room is lit with a small paraffin hand-lamp.

Upon mounting the stairs to the upper story you find two rooms; on the right a double-bedded room, plainly furnished with a mahogany chest of drawers and a dressing-table, the floor covered with oilcloth and several Persian rugs; and on the left a second bedroom, smaller by the space occupied by the staircase, which is so boxed off as to leave a boarded recess above it usable as a lumber-shelf.

This room holds a single bed and dressing-table, and in one corner an incubator. Both rooms are roofed by the gable of the house, which is held together by cross-beams; walls and ceiling alike are paneled (as on the lower story) with match-boarding.

Such is Doarlish Cashen, a dark, lonely, and rather eerie place, last survivor of a whole group of little farms which once flourished upon the downs above Glen Maye. During the prosperous days of the last century it was the home of a rich Frenchman named Pierre Baume, who was eccentric and miserly, but at his death in 1875 left a considerable sum of money to form an educational trust for the encouragement of music studies in the Isle of Man.

Apart from this it has had no remembered history, until in the early days of the Great War it came into the occupation of its present owner, James T. Irving and his remarkable family. On the hills around Doarlish Cashen you may any day see a vigorous white-haired man of sixty-three, of medium height, tending the thirty sheep which form the main stock of his farm of forty-five .acres. His cheerful, weather-beaten countenance bears the hale look of a man who is out in all weathers, who never suffers a day's illness, who enjoys life and seeks contact with his fellow-creatures.

But Irving is no farmer bred to the soil. True, he is of Scottish Border descent; but he himself was born in Lancashire, and followed the profession of commercial traveler. The short, broad fingers of his hands are unstained by heavy manual lahour, and suggest rather the nervous energy of the man of thought. Irving is an educated man, pretty well-read, of wide interests and knowledge of the world. He has picked up a smattering of many languages, particularly German, and knows a few words and phrases of Russian, Arabic, and even Hindustani.

He is a non-smoker and abstemious. Before the war: he represented a Canadian firm of piano manufacturers, from whom he used to receive the then substantial remuneration (including expenses) of six hundred pounds a year. But the war interfered with the Canadian piano trade, and so Irving was forced to seek a livelihood in some other direction.

In 1915, during a visit to Peel in the Isle of Man, where lived relations of Mrs. Irving, he came across Doarlish Cashen, then up for sale at the order of Pierre Baume's executors., Irving invested his savings in the purchase of this property, probably paying for the freehold the sum of several hundred pounds.

(*His former profession used to bring him into contact with many Jews, and he still retains not only a working knowledge of Yiddish, but a curious interest in the race and its ways-exemplified in the Yiddish magical sign which he has painted on one of his fowl-houses.*)

The land was then in fairly good condition, and part of it was leased by the government, for cultivation by a batch of a hundred German prisoners who were interned at Glen Maye. But Irving himself did not at once settle down to a farmer's life. For the first year or two he left matters in charge of his son-who was now grown up-whilst he endeavoured to find new business openings for himself in Liverpool. Only when these failed to materialize did he decide to settle permanently, with Mrs. Irving, at Doarlish Cashen.

Doarlish Cashen, with James Irving and Voirrey outside their front door.

The farm-house itself required considerable repairing and improving to make it comfortable. Irving spent a good deal of his remaining savings on cementing the walls outside to make them weatherproof, paneling the interior walls with matchboarding to keep away draughts and cold, and adding a porch to protect the front door from gales. One of the interned Germans – a carpenter – helped Irving to undertake this paneling work, and also taught him various additions to his German vocabulary. Thus by the end of the war Irving was in fairly prosperous circumstances, with his farm well stocked and well tilled, and his son working for him.

The Irvings had also a married daughter, Elsie, who has unfortunately been left a widow; she did not accompany her parents to Doarlish Cashen, but continued to live in Liverpool. Then in 1918 a second daughter was born, who received the charming name Voirrey – a Manx form of Mary. Voirrey was many years younger than her brother and sister, and has been brought up to know little of the great world beyond the neighbourhood of Glen Maye.

Gradually the flood of post-war prosperity abated, and the ebb tide of farming set in. Prices of farm produce fell; countrymen migrated increasingly to the towns. Irving ceased to employ outside hired labour, and his acreage under the plough shrank. Then, as time went on, his son became restless. Perhaps he felt that opportunities for a young man to make his way in life were sadly scarce in Glen Maye. However that may be, in 1928 he left Doarlish Cashen, turned his back upon the Isle of Man, and migrated to London, where he found himself suitable manual work, and became self-supporting. Today his parents hear from him but rarely.

The departure of young Irving made it difficult to farm Doarlish Cashen as before. Now that no labour was to be had, the land must go back to grass, and Irving must carry on with whatever stock he could manage single-handed – or, rather, with the aid of his womenfolk. And so Doarlish Cashen has become what the visitor finds it now forty-five acres of rough gorse and moss-ridden grass, with nothing but the bare sod hedges to remind one of its former crops.

Irving owns, to be exact, some thirty sheep, four or five goats, a dozen geese, and a few chickens and ducks. Yet even stock-rearing in this desolate country is a perpetual struggle against nature. Sheep and lambs stray, or suffer from attacks by great crows; polecats raid the poultry yard; while if chickens are left unattended in the open for more than ten minutes at a time, they are pounced upon by the fierce hawks which everywhere abound.

However, in the midst of all these difficulties Irving retains his cheerfulness and sense of humour. He is "a good mixer", and above all a mighty talker and raconteur. No man was ever less shut up in himself; indeed, he will regale friends and visitors with an almost embarrassing richness of information concerning his own affairs and adventures. As a farmer he is modest, admitting that nowadays he lives chiefly by selling every season some thirty lambs, the wool off the backs of his sheep, together with sundry rabbits, eggs, and poultry.

He grows no vegetables, but earns a supply of potatoes by occasionally lending a hand on his nearest neighbour's farm. For nine months out of the twelve his household drinks goats' milk, for the rest, tinned milk. Irving has told us that his total money income for last year amounted to no more than thirty-nine pounds; or fifteen shillings a week – truly a slender figure upon which to maintain a wife and growing daughter.

GEF THE TALKING MONGOOSE

If you enter the living-room at Doarlish Cashen, it will be long before you can take your gaze off Mrs. Irving, to outward eye the most striking personality in the household. You see a tallish woman of fifty-nine, of dignified bearing, upright and square of carriage, neatly dressed in the style of a former generation. Her grey hair rises primly above her forehead, to frame her most compelling feature – two magnetic eyes that haunt the visitor with their almost uncanny power.

Mrs. Irving belongs to a type that you would guess at first glance to be "psychic"; she herself believes firmly in her own powers of intuition, and has gifts of seeing more than ordinary mortals see with the outward eye. She is a Manxwoman on the side of her mother, who lived in Peel until her recent death at a great age.

Mrs. Irving is obviously of wiry constitution and strong physique, for throughout her mother's last illness she made frequent, even daily, visits to Peel on foot to see her. Now, the journey to Peel is eight miles return, and begins and ends with the toil-some path between Glen Maye and Doarlish Cashen. In addition, Mrs. Irving is clearly the mainstay of the Irving domestic establishment.

To her meticulous care and constant work the visitor must attribute the order and cleanliness maintained in the farm-house, the good repair of the clothes and furnishing, and the hospitable entertainment extended to friends. Her voice is musical in tone and commands attention. Like the rest of her family, she is well-spoken and well-informed.

The third member of the Irving household is to be found most days out upon the downs, tramping the hillsides above Glen

Maye in solitude, save for her dog. Voirrey is now seventeen, having left school two years or more. Like her parents she is tall and well-built, not holding herself so well as her mother, but promising to look as striking as the latter must have been in her younger days (to judge from her photograph at that time).

Voirrey is light in colouring, with a pink-and-white complexion, and fair hair coiled in plaits behind her ears. She carries something of her mother's strange look in her greenish-brown eyes, which, rarely fully open, seem to observe the world with a penetrating yet half-concealed disdain. This young lady, you would conclude, is old for her years, isolated though those years have been from the ordinary rough and tumble of human experience.

(In common with the other members of her family, Voirrey has a rather strange dislike of broad sunshine, which seems to hurt her eyes.)

She must have passed a curious childhood, without playmates or friends, always in the company of her elderly parents, seeing life from their remote and limited angle. At school she was not exceptionally apt at her lessons, yet she is obviously intelligent and self-possessed. For a young girl she certainly seems undemonstrative, so reserved in fact that you could easily fancy her moody. She is not interested in books, though her father will tell you that she has, or had a great interest in animals and used eagerly to devour any reading upon that subject that might come into the house.

Voirrey's main occupation, in fact, is with the animals of the farm. She is the early riser at Doarlish Cashen, first making her parents their cup of tea, next milking the goats and attending to the poultry, and lastly going her round of the rabbit-snares which Irving has set out overnight in his fields, to see if anything has been caught.

GEF THE TALKING MONGOOSE

There are, of course, household duties to be performed later in the day; but these leave her plenty of time for roaming the hills in search of flowers, bilberries, mushrooms, and so forth.

Voirrey had never, up to the summer of 1935, left the Isle of Man, or indeed visited the northern half of the Isle, beyond Ramsey. Nevertheless, she is rather more sophisticated in her tastes than this fact might lead one to suppose. She is greatly interested, not so much in natural as in mechanical objects, such as motor-cars, aero planes, and cameras. She knows the names and recognizes the leading points of all the principal makes of automobiles. She pays special attention to the local motor-bus routes and their garage, as well as to the flying services between London and the Isle of Man. She can manipulate a hand-camera with 'some skill, and seems to enjoy being photographed.

There is, indeed, a touch of vanity about her character, natural enough in a young lady who has been brought up as an 'only child' in a very real sense. She wears for visitors a silk or cotton frock, a necklace, and a gold signet ring; she has reached the age of using perfume, but not other cosmetics. There remains a fourth (but dumb) member of the Irving household, Mona, the collie or sheep-dog, a pretty animal., with dark brown or black hair, shading off much lighter on the underside of the body. Mona is a charming, friendly creature, only three years old, who does not bark at strangers but plays with them vivaciously upon any excuse.

She is not trained, to round up sheep in the professional style, but Irving claims for her at least one trick of an unusual kind. Rabbit-catching at Doarlish Cashen has its own peculiar technique, as a later chapter in this narrative will show. Here, however, it suffices to repeat Irving's own account of a method evolved by

Voirrey and Mona in collaboration, for catching rabbits without snare or gun. If, in the course of their rambles together (Mona follows Voirrey about everywhere, rather than her father), they come upon a rabbit sitting within view, at a distance of say fifteen or twenty yards, outside the entrance to its burrow, Voirrey will call Mona's attention to the rabbit, where-upon the dog will "point" her prey, and mesmerize it so that it remains stiff and paralysed, and cannot run away. Thereupon Voirrey, leaving Mona to hold the rabbit's attention, will walk round in a circle, come up quietly behind it, and kill it with a well directed blow upon the head. Irving avers that his daughter has many times performed this feat, which must be of great value in helping to stock the modest larder at Doarlish Cashen.

It may be added that Mona, though she sleeps in the porch of the farm-house at night, with the doors leading to the parlour, living-room, and staircase locked, is of no use as a watchdog—a function which the Irvings prefer to entrust to their geese, who usually sleep in the grassy "haggard" (yard) outside.

Such then are the inhabitants of Doarlish Cashen, a sufficiently remarkable family, existing under conditions which could hardly be paralleled anywhere in the British Isles. Their house is remote from the world, on a desolate, windswept down – yet they dress, speak, and behave as though they belonged to ordinary suburbia.

Their farm yields little or no produce, yet they appear to fare in decent comfort without, to apply a hackneyed phrase, possessing much "visible means of subsistence". Most people would find such a way of living nearly intolerable, but it seems to suit the Irvings, who remain a united, cheerful, and healthy trio of normally intelligent persons. Nevertheless, into their lives has entered a mystery, perhaps one of the most curious and unaccountable mysteries of our times. Their solitary farm has become the scene of what is alleged to be a supernatural visitation-such a visitation as was common enough three hundred years ago, when the reality of witches and their familiars was acknowledged and feared.

The haunting of Doarlish Cashen has now continued for over four years, and has been recorded with such detail and circumstance by the Irving family and others that the whole affair lends itself to more thorough examination than is usually possible in such cases. In the following chapters the marvellous story is set forth without embellishment, and analysed in a scientific spirit.

Voirrey Irving, James Irving, R.S. Lambert

CHAPTER II

THE STORY OF THE HAUNTING

NEWS of the mystery first reached London in October 1931, when paragraphs concerning a Manx prodigy called a "man-weasel" appeared in the Press. Thus the *Daily Sketch* published a photograph of Irving's cottage, with the caption "The 'Talking Weasel' Farm", and the *Daily Mail* and other journals briefly reported strange events at Doarlish Cashen. The northern dailies took a greater and more sustained interest in the affair, because the talking animal was a near neighbour, and naturally attracted more attention than he did in London.

Early in 1932 the Manchester *Daily Dispatch* sent a reporter to the Isle of Man in order to investigate the mystery on the spot. Their representative was fortunate in hearing the "weasel" speak on his first visit. We cannot do better than quote his own words as published in the *Dispatch*: "The mysterious 'man-weasel' of Doarlish Cashen has spoken to me today. Investigation of the most remarkable animal story that has ever been given publicity—a story which is finding credence all over the Island leaves me in a state of considerable perplexity. Had I heard a weasel speak? I do not know, but I do know that I have heard to-day a voice which I should never have imagined could issue from a human throat; that the people who claim it was the voice of the strange weasel seem sane, honest, and responsible folk and not likely to indulge in a difficult, long, drawn-out and unprofitable practical joke to make themselves the talk of the world; and that others had had the same experience as myself."

Mr. Irving related to the reporter the story of how the animal had taken up its abode at the farm, but denied that the place was "haunted".

"There are no spooks here," he cried.

The newspaper man was impressed by what he had heard at Doarlish Cashen, especially as the "weasel" gave him a "tip" for the Grand National! But, after sleeping on it, the *Daily Dispatch* representative became apparently less convinced that the manifestations were abnormal, and considered that the "animal" might be a fantasy of Voirrey's childish imagination.

In his next report (published the following day) he says: "Does the solution of the mystery of the "man-weasel" of Doarlish Cashen lie in the dual personality of the 13-year-old girl, Voirrey Irving? That is the question that leaps to my mind after hearing the piercing and uncanny voice attributed to the elusive little yellow beast with a weasel's body. Its alleged powers of speech have caused a widespread sensation…Yesterday I heard several spoken sentences and was told that these noises were made by the 'man weasel'. The conversation was between the 'weasel-voice' and Mrs. Irving, who was unseen to me in another room, while the little girl sat motionless in a chair at the table. I could see her reflection, although not very clearly, in a mirror on the other 'side of the room. She had her fingers to her lips. I kept my eyes on the face in the glass. The lips did not move, so far as I could, see, but they were partly hidden by her fingers. When I edged my way into the room, the voice ceased. The little girl continued to sit motionless, without taking any notice of us. She was sucking a piece of string, I now saw. It is interesting to note that this reporter actually heard the 'voice' when the girl was in his presence, a few feet from him – an experience hardly ever vouchsafed to later witnesses of the phenomenon."

Hard upon the heels of these newspaper reports came a letter to Mr. Harry Price (who was then Director of the National Laboratory of Psychical Research) giving in greater detail an account of the curious manifestations which were puzzling the Manxmen. This was in February 1932. The writer was Miss Florence Milburn, of Glenfaba Road, Peel, and she told an extra- ordinary story.

In her letter (February 12th 1932) she stated that in September 1931 Mr. Irving noticed a strange animal among the fowls in the farmyard. In appearance it was similar to a weasel, with small body, long bushy tail, flat nose, and yellow in colour. Being arrested by its ability to bark like a dog, then mew like a cat, Mr. Irving imitated the cries of various familiar farmyard animals, whereupon the stranger repeated every one correctly without hesitation.

A little while after—Miss Milburn continued—the Irvings heard a loud thumping on the stained wooden match-boarding with which the rooms of their house are panelled, and it proved to be the animal trying to attract attention. The letter contained a good deal more about the 'weasel' and his doings, and Mr. Irving's address was given.

Mr. Price wrote to him. In his reply (February 22nd 1932) Mr. Irving gave a short account of the finding of the animal and a description of the alleged manifestations.

GEF THE TALKING MONGOOSE

He says: "The animal in question has been seen by myself and daughter of 14 (Voirrey), in one of the two bedrooms of my house, on several occasions in the month of October last. My daughter has on two occasions in January 1932 seen its tail only, in the small back kitchen, in a hole in the wall. My wife has seen it on one occasion only in October. The colour is yellow, not too pronounced, after the ferret. The tail is long and bushy, and tinged with brown. In size, it is about the length of a three-parts grown rat in the body, without the tail. It can, and does, pass through a hole of about one and a half inches diameter. I, personally, am strongly inclined to the view that it is a hybrid between a stoat and a ferret. The bushy tail is not that of a stoat, and the size certainly half that of the ferrets I have examined. My daughter says the face is all yellow, and the shape is more that of a hedgehog, but flattened at the snout, after the fashion of the domestic pig."

Mr. Irving stated that though the three members of his family had heard it outside his house, not one of them had ever seen it outside. This account is at variance with the story told by Miss Milburn, who informed Mr. Price that 'the animal was first seen in the farmyard among the chickens'. In the same letter to Mr. Price, Mr. Irving says: "We were first made aware of its presence in September last by its barking, growling, spitting, and persistent blowing, which I understand is the procedure of the weasel family. Now as regards its speaking ability, it did not possess this power until the first week in November last; but now converses, incredible as it is, as rationally as most human beings. Its first sounds were those of an animal nature, and it used to keep us awake at night for a long time as sleep was not possible. It occurred to me that if it could make these weird noises, why not others, and I proceeded to give imitations of the various calls, domestic and other creatures make in the country, and I named these creatures after every individual call. In a few days' time one had only to name the particular animal or bird, and instantly, always without error, it gave the correct call. My daughter then tried it with nursery rhymes, and no trouble was experienced in having them repeated. The voice is quite two octaves above any human voice, clear and distinct, but lately it can and does come down to the range of the human voice. It is not a prisoner, and I have no control whatever over its movements and I can never tell whether it is in or not. It announces its presence by calling either myself or my wife by our Christian names. It apparently can see in' the dark and describe the movements of my hand. Its hearing powers are phenomenal. It is no use whispering: it detects a whisper 15 to 20 feet away, tells you that you are whispering, and repeats exactly what one has said. Mrs. Irving added a footnote to the effect that 'my husband's statements are perfectly correct'".

The Irvings decided to tolerate the animal, though previously the farmer tried to kill it by means of gun, trap, and poison. It eluded all attempts at capture, dead or alive.

It can be imagined that the receipt of the letter caused considerable interest among the officials of the National Laboratory of Psychical Research, and Mr. Price decided to send a representative to Doarlish Cashen in order to make some inquiries on the spot. Captain Macdonald, a well-known racing motorist and business man and a member of the National Laboratory's Council, accordingly crossed to the island and visited the farmstead, where he arrived at 7.30 p.m. on February 26th 1932. He afterwards furnished Mr. Price with a report (dated February 28th 1932), from which the following information has been extracted.

GEF THE TALKING MONGOOSE

MR. R. S. LAMBERT POINTING TO A BREAK IN THE SOD HEDGE
WHERE GEF IS ALLEGED TO LEAVE THE RABBITS HE KILLS

HOLE IN THE OUTSIDE WALL OF DOARLISH CASHEN
THROUGH WHICH GEF IS ALLEGED TO ENTER AND LEAVE THE HOUSE

"I sat in a comer of the living-room, and listened to Mr. and Mrs. Irving again giving me their story, more or less in agreement with what we already had been told. Then they showed me various cracks, and holes in the woodwork of the room which the animal used (so they said) to see who was there. We sat and talked until just about 11:45 p.m. and as nothing had taken place, I suggested making my way back to Glen Maye. Mr. Irving said he thought he had better pilot me home, so we put on our overcoats and set forth. Just as I had shut the door of the house we heard a very shrill voice from inside scream out 'Go away. Who is that man?' Mr. Irving gripped my arm and said: 'That's it!' I heard the shrill voice continuing, but was unable to catch exactly what it was saying. We remained outside for five minutes, but I was so cold that I told Mr. Irving that I must either go in again, or go on down the hill. We decided to go in, so I stalked back, and quietly got in the room, when the voice at once ceased."

Captain Macdonald stayed for fifteen minutes, but hearing nothing further, returned to his hotel at Glen Maye. Next morning (February 27th) Captain Macdonald returned to the farm at 10.30, in order to have a long day with the "weasel", as they still called it. Mr. Irving greeted him with the news that the animal had been talking that morning, and had promised to speak to him in the evening provided that he "made a promise to give Voirrey a camera or gramophone". The report continues:

"I was also informed that I had to sit in a recess in the room as the animal said it had been looking at me the previous night and did not like me; again, it also said that it knew that I did not believe in it, so I would have to shout out in the early evening that I did believe in it, etc."

At 5:30 p.m. Mr. Irving suggested a cup of tea, so Voirrey prepared some, and Captain Macdonald, Mr. Irving, and his daughter sat down at the table (Mrs. Irving had gone to Peel).

"While we were talking, something was thrown from the panel behind Mr. Irving. It struck the teapot, or possibly a cup, and Mr. Irving said: 'That's the animal.' We examined the cloth and found a large packing-case needle, which I picked up and gently threw at the teapot, when exactly the same noise was again made, Mr. Irving saying that it constantly threw things at the family. At 6:15 p.m. we heard plates and similar things being moved in the small scullery. No one was there. A little later, again the same noise, and again no one was there, but we found a little stream of water running from a small hole in the wall, which Mr. Irving said was the animal performing its natural functions. I saw no sign of rats or mice, but Mr. Irving said that there were plenty of weasels about. At 7:20 Mrs. Irving returned from Peel and was astonished to hear that the animal had not spoken, in view of its morning promise."

After waiting a short time Mr. Irving asked his wife to "go upstairs and see if you can make the creature begin", remarking to Captain Macdonald: "If we can get him to start upstairs he will then come into this room." Accordingly, Mrs. Irving and Voirrey went up to the bedroom immediately above the living-room. Captain Macdonald continues.

"In about three minutes there was a shrill scream, Mr. Irving saying: 'There it is.' Then Mrs. Irving said: 'No, come on and talk!' whereupon a very shrill voice started talking in the bedroom, and kept on talking to Mrs. Irving for 15 minutes. I then shouted that as I believed in the animal, would it come down? I received a shrill reply: 'No! I don't mean to stay long as I don't like you!' I then quietly crawled up the dark staircase, but by sheer bad luck, and owing to one of the stairs being broken, I slipped and fell, making a terrible noise – the result being that the shrill voice screamed: 'He is coming!'"

Though Captain Macdonald stayed until midnight, the "voice" was not heard again, and he went back to his hotel. Captain Macdonald concluded his report to Mr. Price by rightly remarking that as Mrs. Irving and her daughter were upstairs when the voice was heard, the evidence for its abnormality 'was not of much value'.

For the next three years (except for a break in 1933) the doings of the animal were faithfully recorded in the form of letters sent to Captain Macdonald. Copies were deposited with the National Laboratory of Psychical Research (which, in June 1934, became the University of London Council for Psychical Investigation). The adventures of the "weasel" might have been taken from the pages of *A Thousand And One Nights*, so remarkable are the fantastic improbabilities which the record contains.

All these adventures were related to the present writers when they visited Doarlish Cashen in July 1935, and what they were told tallies in almost every particular with the incidents recorded in the scores of letters which Captain Macdonald received from Mr. Irving. The following pages chronicle the history of the animal from the first visit of Captain Macdonald in February 1932 to his second investigation in May 1935.

It was in March 1932 that Mr. Irving discovered that the animal was an Indian mongoose. About twenty years previously a farmer named Irvine, whose land was in the vicinity of Doarlish Cashen, procured a number of mongooses which he turned loose in the fields, in order to kill the rabbits. Mr. Irving concluded that his talking mongoose was a descendant, but was afterwards informed by the animal himself that he was born on June 7th 1852, and came from Delhi and had been chased and shot at by natives!

It was about this time that Mrs. Irving saw it outside the house. Voirrey also tried to photograph it, the animal sitting on its hind-quarters and posing for her. The girl not being quick enough, the mongoose vanished. But the farmer was successful in inducing it to eat chocolate, bananas, and potato pie, which were left in convenient spots overnight.

In June 1932 the mongoose became on more familiar terms with his hosts, especially Mrs. Irving. He was persuaded to run on the cross-beams and show himself more. They discovered that his front feet resembled a human hand, with three or four fingers and a thumb, which gripped Mr. Irving's fingers as in a vice. Mrs. Irving, being bolder, stroked his head and back and felt his teeth. This was while the animal was on the cross-beams in the upper part of the house.

At about this period the mongoose began to kill rabbits for the Irving family, perhaps in exchange for his board and lodging. Having killed a rabbit, he would tell Irving where he had placed it-generally in a convenient position near the house.

The mongoose usually called Mr. Irving 'Jim' or 'Pots', and one morning in April 1932 the farmer was awakened at 5 a.m. by the animal calling: "Jim, Jim, I am sick!" and it could be heard vomiting behind the panelling. It was discovered that he had stolen some unsuitable food in a cottage eight miles away. These journeys were not infrequent, and often he would slip away for a few days' "holiday". Sometimes he would bring something home in his mouth: a paint-brush, pair of pincers, a pair of gloves, etc. He informed his hosts that he had found these in the road. He would frequently carry small objects about the house, and throw them into the rooms. He was especially fond of a ball, which he would bounce on top of a boxed partition (his 'sanctum') to the tune of a gramophone.

In the summer of 1932 the Irvings discovered that their guest knew several languages. For example, the animal called out: "Ne pani amato aporusko", which was recorded phonetically. It was supposed to be Russian. Then he sang a line of a Manx hymn: "Moyll jee yor chiarn lest ard choraa." This was taught him by Mr. Irving. The Irvings called their prodigy "Jack". But during the summer of 1932 this was gradually softened to "Gef", and the animal said he liked the name. So, to our readers, the mongoose will henceforth be "Gef".

During the late summer and autumn of 1932 Gef, if we may use the term, "dug himself in", and became an intimate and valued member of the Doarlish Cashen household. Like members of other households, he sometimes became difficult and did not always see eye to eye with Irving's relatives. For example, Mr. Irving has an elder daughter Elsie, and Gef took a violent dislike to her. Elsie is married and sometimes visits her father. But Gef told Mr. Irving quite plainly that if Elsie took up her abode in the cottage he would go away. During Elsie's infrequent visits the animal will not speak. Once he was asked whom he liked best, Mr. Irving, Mrs. Irving, or Voirrey.

"If one of us had to die, which would you prefer?"

He replied: "I do not want any of you to die. I like you all, but don't let us talk about death!"

THE IRVING HOUSEHOLD
Mr. J.T. Irving   Mrs. Irving
Voirrey Irving   Mona, The Sheep-Dog

GEF THE TALKING MONGOOSE

Gef appears to have a real affection for Voirrey. By the end of the year 1932 Gef had become very proficient in killing rabbits for the Irving family, and the faunal equilibrium of the district was in danger of being upset. Often at breakfast time he would call out that he had killed a rabbit, I and give the precise spot where it was to be found. He said he killed them by the throat, and they certainly appeared as if they had been strangled.

Although Gef was very infrequently seen outside of the farm-house during the summer of 1932, he began to absent himself from home. He would take an occasional holiday for a day or so, and, upon his return, he would say where he had been. For example, he visited Ramsey cattle show and stayed away for two days (August 3rd to 5th). Ramsey is twenty miles from Doarlish Cashen. It was again absent from August 9th to 13th.

Though out and about, he was seldom seen on the roads by any of the family. But on October 22nd 1932 he made his presence known by throwing stones at Mrs. Irving as she was returning from Peel. She shouted: "Is that you, Gef?" He answered: "Yes, Maggie the witch woman, the Zulu woman, the Honolulu woman!"

This was rather rude of him, but they excused him because he was so excited at the return of his hostess. A few days later he made amends by finding a lamb that Irving had lost. It was found exactly at the spot that Gef had indicated.

By Christmas 1932 Mr. Irving had discovered that the forefeet of Gef were much larger than the hind feet. Not only were they larger, but they had the appearance of human hands, with extensile fingers. He gathered these facts from impressions in the dust which the animal made during his nocturnal rambles about the house. Gef admitted that he had three long fingers and a thumb, and said they were "as large as a big doll's hands". The fact that he frequently picks up such small and flat objects as coins, pins, etc., rather points to his having some sort of fingers on his forefeet. A set of paw prints in plasticine and dough which the present writers received after their visit confirms Gef's statements. Not only does he claim to have hands rather like human beings, but he uses them in the same way. "Doubters" (those who do not believe in Gef) are painfully aware of this, as small objects, stones, etc., are thrown at them if they do not "believe". As a variant Gef sometimes spits at them through a crack!

If Gef is a mongoose, his food is decidedly that of humans. Captain Macdonald sent Voirrey a box of chocolates. Gef, with his eye to a squint-hole, saw the box arrive. A little later, when Mr. Irving asked Gef if he were hungry, he said: "Yes, I will have some of Captain Macdonald's chocolates; a nut and a black paradise and a muck sweet!"

To Gef, "muck sweets" are the plain boiled sugar sweets, highly coloured. Gef refuses to touch mongoose food.

Gef celebrated the New Year of 1933 by absenting himself from home. He would often spend an entire week away from Doarlish Cashen. Once he said he had been to the omnibus depot at Peel, hiding under the floor, and listening to what the men were saying. He returned to the farm and told the family about his adventure, and repeated some phrases in the Manx tongue. On his next visit to Peel, Irving called at the depot and was told that an old man had been there, speaking the Manx language – a linguistic feat only one Manxman in five hundred is capable of. Gef frequently visits Peel and tells the Irvings what the people there have been doing and saying. On one occasion, it is alleged, Gef accurately described what a man and his wife had for their supper, and what their conversation was about.

There is a curious hiatus in Irving's record of Gef's life at Doarlish Cashen, as chronicled in letters to Captain Macdonald. The break in his diary' lasted from February 1933 until April 1934. The mongoose was not lying dormant or anything like that: the farmer simply omitted to inform the Captain of the daily doings of his prodigy. As a matter of fact, Gef was very much alive and active during 1933, and, as Mr. Irving pointed out when he resumed the correspondence, "Our joint and various experiences are too wonderful for words". He confirmed this when he discussed the 1933 period with us.

During the year 1933 Gef became much tamer. It allowed Mrs. Irving to place her finger in his mouth and feel his teeth. He also shook hands with his hostess, when the three long fingers and a thumb were plainly seen. She told her husband that he gripped her hand like a vice. Mrs. Irving also saw him once out of doors, and her husband, on different occasions, caught two glimpses of him as he swiftly darted across a gap in one of the sod hedges with which the farm is surrounded. The animal was distinctly annoyed at being seen and on both occasions called out: "I did not intend you to see me. Out of friends for seeing me!"

Though so seldom seen outside the cottage, he was often to be found squatting on the cross-beams of the roof. It was here that he took his food: chocolates, bananas, biscuits, lean bacon, sausages, potato pie, etc. Though sitting on the beam, the animal was careful not to expose the whole of his body at one time. He said he was desperately afraid of being caught.

GEF THE TALKING MONGOOSE

It was during 1933 that Mr. Irving confirmed his opinion that the animal could read. From a squint-hole behind the panelling Gef would call out the name of any book, newspaper, or periodical that a member of the household might be reading, and he was always right. Once Mr. Irving was reading the *Liverpool Post* when Gef shrieked out: "I see something!" Upon being asked what had disturbed him he said: "I see a name that makes me quake, that makes me shake!" Irving scanned the paper, but could see nothing that might have alarmed the animal, who again cried out: "Look in the deaths!" Irving did so, and found that a man named Jeffery had died. In brackets was the word "Jef". This coincidence had not been noticed until the mongoose screamed his fright.

At about this time it was discovered that Gef could understand the deaf and dumb language. Out of curiosity, Mr. Irving made signs with his fingers and the animal guessed the word before it was completed. Another word was tried, but Gef exclaimed: "Do it again. You went too hellish quick!"

Another faculty which, it is alleged, Gef developed in 1933 was a sort of clairvoyant one. For example, if Mr. Irving happened to be returning from Peel, Gef would prognosticate his arrival at the cottage to a minute. When her husband was half a mile away Gef would exclaim to Mrs. Irving: "Jim is coming" and "Jim" always came. This was so uncanny that it was suggested to him that he was a spirit. He denied the soft impeachment and explained that he did it by "magic". "If I were a spirit, I could not kill rabbits," was his argument. And he continued to kill rabbits, which, after strangling with his hands, he left at convenient spots. Usually the rabbits were on their backs with their four feet in the air. But Gef cannot be relied upon to tell his hosts exactly what he is, as at various times he has called himself a "tree", a "mongoose', a "marsh mongoose", and an "earth-bound spirit". This last description is a purely spiritualistic term. The Irvings think that he is afraid of death.

Gef suddenly took to singing and speaking in strange tongues. We are told that "the voice is extremely high pitched, above the human range, with a clear, sweet tone". Sometimes, in the still of the evening, Irving would hear Gef softly practising the Tonic Sol-fa scale. Then he would sing a hymn or two, or a song. It is thought that he picked up the Tonic Sol-fa at a local school which, apparently, he attended for singing lessons. He began to sing more and more: songs, hymns, and ballads. Some of these the Irvings knew, some were new to them. His singing became almost a nuisance. Later, he danced on top of his "sanctum" to the tune of a gramophone record.

There is still some doubt as to Gef's antecedents, and where he was before attaching himself to the Irving household. He said he came from Delhi; and, to test him, Irving asked him to speak Hindustani. The following list of words spoken by the animal at various times was sent to us in September 1935. The vocabulary is not an extensive one, and some of the words are familiar even to schoolchildren: Allah, ballah, bigontee, tishoo, charboo, Yogi, punkah, rani, maharajah, nabob, etc. It is curious that Gef knows so little of any Indian language, and so much English-and Manx. Once, when Irving was not very quick at hearing something the mongoose said, Gef retorted: "You are as thick in the head as a lump of kauri!" Irving states that the word kauri is a Maori word for a tree and its gum. It is apparent that Irving must have used this word in conversation with his family, and that Gef thus learnt it from him.

It has been mentioned that, from his hiding place behind the panelling, Gef is able to peruse journals, letters, etc., while being read by the Irvings. But it was discovered that he also does a little independent reading of newspapers, perhaps when the family has retired for the night. The question was raised whether Mr. Price should accompany Captain Macdonald on his next visit. Immediately Gef heard their names he screamed out: "The two spook men!" and began to make fun of the name "Price". Of course, this was not difficult even for an educated mongoose. Then he called out: "Ask Harry Price whose was the invisible hand that scattered the violets about the room at night". He continued: "You know, Olga and Rudi Schneider."

Irving declares that although he had seen in the press an account of Mr. Price's investigation of Rudi Schneider, the incident of the violets and the alleged spirit hand was quite unknown to him. But an account of this particular séance had appeared in May 7, 1932 edition of *The Times* and other papers, and apparently Gef had read all about it. Although the mongoose had never been introduced to Mr. Price, and did not know him except by repute, Gef appeared a little afraid of him. When it was suggested that both Mr. Price and Captain Macdonald should visit Doarlish Cashen, Gef said that the Captain was welcome, "but not Price. He's got his doubting cap on!" In October 1934 another reference was made to Mr. Price: "I like Captain Macdonald, but not Harry Price. He's the man who puts the kybosh on the spirits!" He also said that he had seen Price's photograph in the papers "and did not like him". But psychical research is not the only subject which Gef studies in the press. As we have seen in the first chapter, Voirrey has an intimate knowledge of the various makes of motor-cars, and takes a great interest in them. So, apparently, does Gef. He worried the life out of Irving as to the make of car owned by Captain Macdonald (who is a well-known motorist). "Was it a 40 H.P. Rolls- Royce Phantom"? It would be interesting to know whether Gef acquired his interest in cars from Voirrey, or vice versa.

Gef is careful not to kill rabbits out of season. By June 1934 he had accounted for forty-seven, and then stopped, owing to their breeding and the warm weather. But as the animal wished to make himself useful during the close season, he busied himself with finding the eggs which Irving's ducks laid in out-of-the-way places all over the farm. Having laid the eggs, the ducks promptly covered them up. But clever Gef nosed around and smelt them out, uncovered them, and reported to Mr. Irving the precise positions where they were to be found. The farmer complimented the animal on his industry and sagacity, and remarked: "What is a leprechaun?" "A goblin," replied Gef. "And what is a pookaun?" "Another kind of goblin," said Gef, who, it will be gathered, knows something about Irish folklore.

If laughter indicates happiness, Gef must be supremely contented in the bosom of the Irving family on that lonely Manx upland. He laughs all day. He possesses an extensive repertoire of laughs. To quote Irving's description: "Sometimes it resembles the tittering laugh of a precocious or mischievous child; at other times I would say it was the chuckling laugh of an aged person, and another distinct type is one which I would say was satanic laughter, or the laughter of a maniac. We all have a most intense dislike to this last laughter, as it is very trying. But, fortunately, we do not get this kind very often."

Sometimes his laughing is not very sympathetic. Mr. Irving was complaining of a minor ailment when the animal "laughed like the very devil" and said: "Hey, Jim, I've got 'joint evil' in my tail." This particular complaint is common to young foals, and Gef must have acquired the expression from the farmer. His knowledge of medical terms is considerable, and once he reeled off the names of some rather obscure diseases. And he is not unacquainted with the *British Pharmacoproeia.* Returning from one of his rambles in the fields, he remarked that he had just consumed a young partridge. Mrs. Irving said she did not believe him. Gef retorted: "I will vomit it up if you will give me some ipec wine!"

It is rare for Gef to get his meals out, and after one of his prolonged trips he returns home famished. In July 1934 he was away for four whole days. The family wondered if he were ever coming back. Mr. Irving had just retired for the night when he was startled by a rapid succession of blows on the panelling just behind his head. (Mrs. Irving was downstairs and Voirrey was in bed.) The blows made the room vibrate. Suddenly a squeaky voice cried out: "Hullo, everybody!" Irving pretended to take no notice. More blows behind his head. At last the farmer spoke to Gef, who shrieked out: "You devil, you heard me before!" Just at that moment Mrs. Irving entered the bedroom and chided Gef, asking why he had stayed away for so long, and why he had returned. The mongoose replied rather perkily: "Well, it's my home!" adding, "What about my chukko?" (meaning food). So Mrs. Irving fetched him some lean bacon and biscuits and placed them on a beam within his reach. The farmer and his wife could hear him munching the biscuits and talking at the same time.

According to the Irvings, an outstanding feature of this remarkable case is Gef's ability to thump the panelling all over the house from, apparently one spot. When he is annoyed or wishes to attract attention, he bangs the wooden boards of each room in quick succession and with lightning rapidity. The fact that the whole house is panelled, and that there is a space of some inches between the boards and the walls (which are two feet six inches thick) means that the interior of the house is like a vast speaking-tube, with panels like drumheads.

It must be extremely difficult to determine the exact location of any sound made inside the house. The Irvings found it difficult to locate Gef's voice at anyone moment, and, when they speak to him, they just talk to the four walls (unless he happens to be visible on a beam). Sometimes when Mr. Irving is speaking to the animal his (the farmer's) eyes will unconsciously rest on that part of the panelling behind which Gef is hiding. Then Gef becomes very perturbed and cries out: "You're looking! Stop looking! Turn your head, you bastard!" (Sometimes Gef is very vulgar.) When asked for an explanation, he said: "I cannot stand your eyes!" But the animal appears very fond of the farmer and sometimes wheedles him into giving him food, unknown to Mrs. Irving.

Occasionally, when his host retires to bed first, Gef, from somewhere behind the panelling, will ask in a low voice: "Hey, Jim, what about some grubbo?" If no notice is taken, the animal gives a terrific thump on the boards. When given a few biscuits he will talk with his mouth full, and throw crumbs at Voirrey in bed in the next room. Throwing small objects at people (especially 'doubters') is a favourite diversion with this very intelligent mongoose.

I think we have remarked that Gef is clever with his hands, or rather paws. Also, he knows a few tricks. One of these is to tell whether a penny is head or tail uppermost when placed in the deep recess which forms the small window of the porch. Some visitor (a "doubter" for preference) is invited to place a penny in the recess and return to the living-room. From a squint-hole in the roof of the porch, Gef squeaks out whether it is a head or a tail. Sometimes he is right.

Another sleight-of-paw trick which the mongoose has acquired is to lock persons in Voirrey's bedroom. The room has a latch which it is alleged can be operated only from the outside. Both Mr. Irving and Voirrey have been locked in, and Captain Macdonald was the victim of a similar joke during his second visit to Cashen's Gap in May 1935. But an even more remarkable trick was performed by Gef in July 1934. There was some sort of "tiff" between Mrs. Irving and the animal, who, as a peace-offering, went hunting for a rabbit to give to his hostess. He was determined to be friendly again and said: "If Mam will speak to me, I will sing two songs for her", and that he had a little present for her. The gift was two biscuits, taken out of a packet in a locked cupboard, which he threw at Mrs. Irving as she lay in bed that same night. Mrs. Irving was not appeased, and the animal remained in her bad books.

A few days later, when the farmer was again in bed, and his wife had not yet joined him, Gef shouted out something. Mrs. Irving heard him, and called up the staircase: "Don't answer him." Gef then said in a faint whisper: "Hey, Jim, what about some grubbo? I'm hungry!" This touching appeal to the farmer was too much for him, so he called out to his wife to bring the animal a couple of biscuits. She did so and threw them on top of Gef's "sanctum" on the top of the boxed-in staircase which is in Voirrey's room. Voirrey was in bed, and the room was in darkness.

For some minutes they could hear Gef groping for the biscuits with his bony fingers. In a plaintive voice the animal said he could not find them (though at other times he can, apparently, see in Stygian darkness). Mrs. Irving said: "Shall I give you a match?"

He said: "Yes, pass them to me." To do this she had to stand on Voirrey's bed. She did so, and Gef took the box out of her hand. He opened it, extracted a match, lit it, said he had found the biscuits, blew the match out, and threw the box into the room. Then he burst out laughing. A few moments later he could be heard munching the biscuits.

Although the Irvings had had Gef literally under their roof for nearly three years, they had by no means sounded the depths of his capabilities. He was always springing surprises on them. Even though they knew he could do a little in the way of foreign languages, they were not prepared for the linguistic treat that was in store for them Jon the evening of July 26th 1934. In succession, Gef sang three verses of "Ellan Vannin", the Manx National Anthem, "in a clear and high-pitched voice"; then two verses in Spanish; followed by one verse in Welsh; then a prayer in pure Hebrew (not Yiddish); finishing up with a long peroration in Flemish. This is not bad going for a creature that knows so little of his own native language.

In addition to his linguistic abilities Gef is something of an arithmetician. One evening he told Irving that Voirrey had been on the Peel bus seven times in a fortnight, the fare being three pence per ride. "Seven threes are twenty- one, and twenty-one pence are one and nine-pence." Then Mrs. Irving suggested that he should be tried with other sums. "How many shillings are a hundred and eighty pence?" said Irving. "Fifteen," said the mongoose, with only a second's hesitation. Then: "How many pence in seventeen and sixpence?" In a few seconds Gef answered: "Two hundred and ten pence."

The farmer remarked that the animal was a long time calculating. Gef replied: "My rectophone wasn't working!" Mr. Irving put to him a question that he thought would not be answered: "How many pence in a guinea?" Gef instantly replied: "Two hundred and fifty-two."

So far the reader has seen only one side of Gef's nature, that of a clever, mischievous, affectionate, and rather wayward little mongoose. But there is another side to his character, and a less pleasant one. In fact, if he pleases, he can be decidedly objectionable. For example, on one occasion he became so violent in his language towards Voirrey that her bed was moved into her parents' room in case the animal should do her an injury. This was in December 1931, a few months after Gef took up his abode in the farm-house. Voirrey returned to her own room in May 1932. The mongoose was then thought to be a malevolent spirit in animal form.

A few weeks before this incident (November 1931), when the father and daughter had retired to rest in their respective rooms (Mrs. Irving was away from home) they both heard a diabolical scream from behind the panelling. Voirrey called to her father to know if he had heard it. He replied that he had put some rat-poison on top of the "sanctum", and that the animal must have consumed some of it.

The screaming continued for more than twenty minutes without ceasing, and then stopped. Mr. Irving said the screaming was as loud as or louder as any human being could make, and reminded him of a pig having its nose "ringed". He was so sure that the animal was dead that some of the panelling in the ceiling was removed and Voirrey was sent into the roof to explore. Nothing was found, and the animal appeared quite all right soon afterwards. On another occasion, when the three Irvings were in bed, loud sighs and moans were heard for more than thirty minutes: they were as if a person was in extreme agony. When asked why he made such a noise, Gef replied: "I did it for devilment!"

During the first few months of his sojourn at Doarlish Cashen, the Irvings more than once seriously considered vacating the place because the animal was so objectionable. That did not cause Gef to mend his ways. His answer to their threats was always: "I am a ghost in the form of a weasel, and I will haunt you!" Eventually the mongoose became better behaved and more affectionate, and is now terrified if Irving mentions anything about their leaving the farm.

By the end of 1934 the Irvings had come to the conclusion that there was some nexus between Voirrey and the mongoose; a sort of mutual affection which made the animal contented with his life at the farm. They also formed the theory that, in some way, Gef's ability to speak at all was due to some power which he drew from the girl, or which she externalized. But, very seriously, Gef seldom speaks to the girl when she is by herself. Usually, one of her parents is with her. The part that Voirrey is alleged to play is a familiar one to students of psychical research, and can be paralleled in nearly every poltergeist case. As a matter of fact, it has been hinted that Gef is a poltergeist in animal form, and that Voirrey is a medium. Some colour is lent to this story by the fact that the manifestations commenced just about the time that the girl reached the age of puberty, and has continued during adolescence. For the story to end in the traditional manner, the "phenomena" should cease, or shortly cease, as Voirrey is now a young woman.

Such mediums as Eleanore Zugun, the Schneider boys, Stella C., etc., lost their powers – real or alleged – when fully developed. When the authors of this work visited Doarlish Cashen in July 1935, there appeared to be little affection between Voirrey and the animal. She denied that she was particularly interested in Gef, and remarked that she would be glad if he left the house. "He is a nuisance," she said.

Though Voirrey states that she has no great love for Gef, she has seen more of the animal than any other person. She has seen him many times, and has even photographed him. Also, she has seen all of him. On the other hand, her parents have often pleaded with the animal to show himself fully, and have always been refused. They sometimes see a portion of him sitting on a beam, or glimpse something flashing past a gap in the hedge, and that is about all. When they ask him to come into the open, they are met with some such excuse as: "I am a freak. I have hands and I have feet, and if you saw me you'd faint, you'd be petrified, mummified, turned into stone, or a pillar of salt!" Gef must have attended Sunday school somewhere!

Gef talks most when the Irving family is in bed and the lights are extinguished. It has been stated that his "sanctum" is in Voirrey's room, and from this "rostrum" he shouts out the events of the day: what he has been doing and what others have been doing. This small-talk is not always acceptable to Mr. and Mrs. Irving, and it keeps Voirrey awake. On one occasion he started screaming out at 11 p.m. and talked incessantly until 3 a.m. No one could sleep, and Irving told him to go. Gef replied: "I am not going to do what you wish. I can stay till 5 if I like!" However, the animal took compassion on them, and in five minutes squeaked out "Vanished!" – his signal that he is about to depart. They heard him jump from the "sanctum" to the floor. Sometimes, when he is tired, he gives a yawn that can be heard all over the house.

Gef's attitude to strangers is one of frightened aloofness. Very occasionally he will speak sensibly to them. But usually he refuses to speak at all, but throws pins or stones at them, and sometimes spits through a crack in the panelling. When they have departed he makes fun of them, calls them "doubters" (or something worse) and criticizes their personal appearance.

On the rare occasions when he speaks to Irving's visitors he is often rude. In November 1934, a South African spiritualist and her friend visited the farm. Mr. Irving and Voirrey were away from home. When they returned Gef was persuaded to say a few words and do the "penny trick". Then he was asked to step into the room (he was behind the panelling somewhere). His answer to this invitation was: "No damned fear; you'll put me in a bottle!" When Gef heard that the lady was going back to South Africa, he cried: "Tell her I hope the propeller drops off!"

Soon after Gef's rudeness to the spiritualist, Mr. Irving was awakened one night by, apparently, someone with a bad fit of coughing. He called out to his daughter to know if it were she who had awakened him. But Voirrey was fast asleep. Then a plaintive little voice came from the "sanctum": "It was me coughing, Jim." Irving asked Gef if he would like a peppermint. The mongoose said "Yes", so a couple was thrown up to him and he could be heard groping for them in the dark. In a few moments he called out that he had found them. Mr. Irving informed the writers that Gef's coughing was "absolutely human".

Gef can be nice enough when he is ill, but the mood does not last. Sometimes gratitude gives place to rudeness. For example, not long after the last incident, Mrs. Irving became possessed of an old Bible. One night her husband was examining this book when Gef (who must have had his eye to a squint-hole) shouted out: "Hey, Maggie, look at the pious old atheist reading the Bible, and he'll be swearing in a minute!" On another occasion he called Mr. Irving a "heathen' and infidel".

When feeling angered at something that Mrs. Irving had said, the animal would shout from his sanctum: "Nuts! Put a sock in it! Chew coke!" This particular bit of rudeness was while the Irvings were in bed. Because no one took any notice of him, he dropped behind the panelling at the head of their bed and gave a terrific thump on the woodwork that shook the place. Two heavy blows followed, but these were in other parts of the house. Mr. Irving told us that the three blows were given in a fraction of a second and immediately after, a box of matches was thrown on their bed. Then the fit of temper passed, and to make amends, Gef asked permission to sing two verses of "The Isle of Capri". This was followed by another song, "Home on the Range", and then a parody on the same song, which he had picked up from the men at the bus depot. This was really too much for Mrs. Irving, who called out: "You know, Gef, you are no animal!" To which the mongoose replied, "Of course I am not! I am the Holy Ghost!" The next morning he drew the outline of his hand in lead pencil on a sheet of, paper. Incidentally, he took the paper from a sideboard cupboard in the living-room, and the pencil out of a drawer. He used the kitchen table as a drawing-board.

The Irvings have often discussed leaving Doarlish Cashen for some more congenial locality. Whenever Gef hears these conversations he says in a pathetic voice: "Would you go away and leave me?"

Voirrey and James Irving.

Mrs. Irving: "Yes, you have not helped us."

Gef: "I got rabbits for you."

Mrs. Irving: "You promised to help us to make money, and you have not done so."

Gef: "No. If you make money, you'll go away and leave me."

Of course Mrs. Irving was joking, but Gef pretends to be deeply concerned when there is any talk of leaving the place. Perhaps this is because of the good living which he receives under the Irvings' hospitable roof. He closely scrutinizes the groceries which are brought in, and once he said to Mrs. Irving: "I know a secret!" Asked what it was, he spelt out "A-p-r-o-c-o-t-s" in reference to a tin of apricots which had just been purchased, and which had been put in a cupboard. Only Mrs. Irving and Gef knew they were there.

About this period (February 1935) Captain Macdonald was making inquiries as to whether he should pay a second visit to Doarlish Cashen. Gef was implored to promise to reveal himself if the Captain should decide to come. But the mongoose would not promise anything, and, in a burst of temper, exclaimed: "I'll go to his house and smash the windows with my fist, and those I cannot reach with my hands I'll break with a picture-pole!" To Mr. Irving's question as to what was a "picture-pole", Gef retorted: "You know damned well what it is!" He added that the farmer could "write and tell Captain Macdonald I said so and I'll go and haunt him". Mr. Irving said the animal could depart and that the family would be well rid of him – a remark which drew forth a plaintive: "I'm not friends with you Jim!" A few nights later he volunteered the information that he had "three attractions". He said: "I follow

Voirrey; Mam gives me food; and Jim answers my questions." The Irvings state that that correctly sums up the situation.

When Gef is in a good mood he sometimes plays tricks on the Irvings. About the middle of February 1935, just as the family had gone to bed, he found an electric torch on top of a bookcase. He seized it, jumped up to his "sanctum" (a distance of three and a half feet) and amused himself by flashing the light on to the Irvings as they lay in bed, switching it on and off, and laughing heartily. To direct the rays from the "sanctum" (which is in Voirrey's room) it was necessary for him to shine the light through an aperture in the wall eight feet from the floor. Asked how he procured the lamp, he replied: "Ah! That's magic!" Two nights later he could not find his biscuits on top of the "sanctum", so Irving told him to fetch the torch and hunt for them. This he did, and switched the light on and off in high glee, finally exclaiming (with his mouth full): "I've got the biscuits".

About this period the Irvings thought that Gef must be able to ventriloquize, or that he could speak in one part of the house while his body was somewhere else. As an example of this, the farmer relates a story of how he and his daughter were in the living-room, with Gef speaking just over their heads, telling them exactly what was happening to Mrs. Irving in another room, twenty-five feet away.

It has also been put on record by Mr. Irving that Gef can, apparently, transform himself into a cat. Soon after Gef attached himself to the family, the farmer saw a large stray cat, striped like a tiger, outside the house; it was a tailless Manx cat. Mr. Irving fetched his gun and followed the cat, which crossed the yard and turned the corner of a sod hedge into a field. When Irving reached the hedge the cat had vanished. There were neither bushes nor stones behind which the animal could have hidden, and the field was quite flat. When Mr. Irving was relating the incident to his wife that same evening, Gef squeaked out: "It was me you saw Jim!"

Upon another occasion Gef took a cigarette from a bedroom and, a little later, threw it over the hedge at Irving. In March 1935 the authors of this work received their first "gift" from Gef. At the request of Mrs. Irving, the animal pulled some fur off his back, some off his tail, and a few dark hairs from the end of his tail. This was done during the night, and Gef placed the "exhibits" in a bowl in the living-room. Then the mongoose called out: "Look in the ornament on the mantelshelf and you will see something frail." Mrs. Irving looked, and found the fur. This was sent to Captain Macdonald, who asked Mr. Price to identify it. Mr. Price sent the hair to Professor Julian Huxley, who handed it to Mr. F. Martin Duncan, F.Z.S., the authority on hair and fur, for identification. At last we had concrete evidence as to the existence of some animal whose coat was composed of varying shades of brown and black fur, some fine, some coarse. Mr. Martin Duncan went to a great deal of trouble and spent much time in identifying the specimens handed to him. In a letter (April 23rd 1935) to Mr. Price he says:

"I have carefully examined them microscopically and compared them with hairs of known origin in my collection. As a result, I can very definitely state that the specimen hairs never grew upon a mongoose, nor are they those of a rat, rabbit, hare, squirrel, or other rodent, or from a sheep, goat, or cow. I am inclined to think that these hairs have probably been taken from a longish-haired dog or dogs – the sample contains hairs of two different thicknesses, though this may only represent upper and under coat. Domestic dogs are not well represented in my collection, of furs, which is composed chiefly from material we have in the Zoological Society's gardens; therefore, I feel only disposed to suggest rather than make a definite decision, as I have had to base my opinion upon a comparison of the hairs of the wolf and of a collie dog. I did find, however, that both these, in the shape and pattern of the cuticular scales and medulla of your specimens, sufficiently close to make me think that very probably yours are of canine origin. One point that might be of interest, though trivial at first sight: I could not detect in the hand a single hair showing the root-bulb, which rather points to their having been cut off their animal owner. When you, visit the farm, keep a look-out for any dog or other domestic animal about the place with a slightly curly hair and of the fawn and dark colour of your sample; and if opportunity occurs that you can gather a few hairs, it might be worth doing.

A few days later (June 3rd 1935) Mr. Martin Duncan again wrote Mr. Price. He said:

"I have now much pleasure in sending you photomicrographs of your 'talking mongoose' hairs, and of hairs from a Golden Cocker Spaniel and a Red Setter. All photographed at x 350 by my special method for demonstrating the cuticular scales. If you will look at these carefully, I think you will agree that there is little doubt that the 'talking mongoose' hairs originated on the body of a dog."

How correct Mr. Martin Duncan was in his opinion will be seen as this story develops. In the spring of 1935, serious attempts were made to photograph Gef, usually by Voirrey. After refusing to "pose" for several days, he finally gave his consent (April 6th 1935) and promised to show himself in the haggart (stackyard). He was asked where Voirrey was to stand. He answered: "How the devil do I know? On the top of her head, if she likes!" in a very surly manner.

The morning for the photograph arrived, but Gef disappeared for some hours. He returned the same evening, asked for biscuits, refused to eat them (because they were of the "afternoon tea" variety), saying: "You can keep them. I don't like them." Then the mongoose disappeared for some days, returned, and again promised to sit for his photograph on Sunday, April 14th. He promised to sit on the haggart wall "with his tail curled up, over his back".

Sunday was fine and Voirrey kept her appointment with the mongoose. But instead of posing for her, he ran along the top of the wall at great speed with his tail in a straight line with his body. Voirrey pressed the button, but, being unused to the camera, did not snap him. As Gef jumped off the wall, he called out: "I'm not coming out again!" This was the first time that anyone had seen Gef so closely or so fully; and Voirrey was asked what he looked like, especially as regards size. She stated that he was rather less than an ordinary ferret, and that the speed at which he ran was "terrific". A further attempt was made on May Day (because Gef was in a congenial mood), when Voirrey persuaded the animal to sit on all fours with his tail over his back, in which position he was snapped. But all these efforts to secure Gef's portrait were futile, as nothing whatever appeared on the film when developed.

Gef has a good memory and he informed his hosts that he was born 'in India'. But he refuses to speak much about his early life; the few details the Irvings have gleaned are either contradictory or false. It was his eighty-third birthday on June 7th 1935, but nothing appears to have been done m the way of celebrating it.

Early in May 1935 Gef pulled some more fur out of his back, and from the tip of his tail. Mr. Irving was away, and his wife had been worrying the mongoose for some more specimens. The animal said he would oblige her, if certain questions were answered. Mrs. Irving promised to do this and, later, Gef called out that there was a "present" in a bowl on the kitchen shelf. He said: "It is very precious." Upon looking into the bowl Mrs. Irving found the fur. Two days later he placed more fur and hair in the bowl, and his contribution included a long, thickish, black hair. Gef said he pulled it out of his eyebrow, and: "Oh, God! It did hurt!' All the new specimens of fur, etc., were sent to Mr. Martin Duncan for identification. His report was that they came from a dog. He said: "The so-called eyebrow is obviously one of the vibrisae,' i.e. the coarse hairs to be found about the mouth of mammals (e.g. the "whiskers" of a cat or dog).

Gef is loyal. On Jubilee Day (May 6th 1935), at breakfast, he informed the family that he was going to Rushen (ten miles away) to celebrate. He promised to let them know what transpired, and the songs that were sung. When he returned he was in a very jovial mood and gave the Irvings a detailed account of the festivities. He said that there were four men there broadcasting, and gave the names of three of them. The account in the local Press confirmed Gef's story. The animal must have been very much behind the scenes as he gave the private conversation between the broadcasters, such as: "Shall we put on Handel's 'Largo'?" and "You've dropped your fountain pen", "The current won't last out till 9.30." These remarks, apparently, were not confirmed. It would be interesting to know why the "current would not last out". It rather suggests that the broadcasters were using batteries of some sort.

The reader is now acquainted with the doings, sayings, and history of the "talking mongoose" down to the period of the middle of May 1935. The record has been compiled from what Mr. Irving told the present writers (during their visit to Doarlish Cashen in July-August 1935), and from what Captain Macdonald related to Mr. Price during the three years that he (the Captain) was receiving letters from the Isle of Man. Mr. Irving's narrative, oft repeated to the authors (who took copious notes), tallies with what he put in his letters.

The letters which Captain Macdonald received from Doarlish Cashen prompted him to make another (his second) visit to the island. The accounts of the diverse, and diverting, "miracles" which were of daily occurrence in the farmstead were so intriguing that the Captain thought he might be lucky enough to witness some of the wonders which his correspondent had recorded from day to day. Accordingly, he wrote Mr. Irving to the effect that he would visit the family on May 20th 1935. He asked Mr. Irving to impress upon Gef the necessity of showing himself during his visit. The Captain pointed out that it would be too bad if his journey of several hundred miles were to be wasted, and he emphasized that it was important that an independent witness should be available in order to support the evidence of the Irving family.

Gef was informed of the impending visit of Captain Macdonald, and he appeared pleased. He became very lively and talkative, a fact which prompted Mrs. Irving to remark: "I wish you would talk like that to Captain Macdonald when he comes." Gef retorted: "He's damned well not going to get to know my inferior complex!" – a remark which rather suggests that the mongoose did not know the meaning of the words he was using. Mrs. Irving replied: "You ought to feel honoured that Captain Macdonald will take the trouble to come all this way to hear you, and especially as he is the only one who believes in you and understands what you actually are." Gefthen remarked: "I might tell him some of my history, but I will not tell him all." He then sang one verse of "Ellan Vannin", which, we are told, was rendered in a "voice that was extremely high-pitched, the tone sweet and clear, quite above the human range".

Captain Macdonald duly arrived at the farm on May 20th, and left on May 23rd 1935. He did not make a report of what took place during his visit, but Mr. Irving prepared one and sent it to the Captain, who passed it on to Mr. Price. The fact that Mr. Irving wrote this report makes it of little value as independent evidence. However hard the farmer tried to make the account impartial and accurate, the fact remains that it is an ex parte report written by the chief supporter of the "mongoose". But it was accepted in good faith by the Captain, who assured the writers that Irving's account is an accurate version of what took place. It may be accurate, but it is a thousand pities that the alleged incidents were not recorded at the time, and on the spot, by the Captain himself.

Captain Macdonald arrived at Cashen's Gap at about 7 p.m. on Monday, May 20th 1935. Tea was served immediately after, and of course the conversation was of Gef, who had not been heard since morning. Quoting from Irving's report (dated May 24th) to Captain Macdonald: "As the evening was getting on, it was necessary for Voirrey to leave the house to feed two or three sitting hens in the stackyard, go to 100 feet away."

When the girl was out of the house, those in the living room heard Gef scream and say something, which was incoherent. Voirrey returned soon after and asked them whether they had heard Gef scream out the one word "Sapphire!"

Irving continues: "This use of the word puzzled us, until, without speaking, you lifted your hand off the table and showed a ring on your finger. You then took the ring off, and allowed us to see it, and I then saw it was a sapphire."

There is something comic about this sapphire' incident. The most casual observer, when meeting Captain Macdonald, cannot help noticing that he wears a ring in which is set a large sapphire. The Captain had visited the farm on a previous occasion, and the ring must have been noticed then, as it certainly was during his second visit. That same night, after Captain Macdonald had gone, Gef was asked how he knew he was wearing a ring. He said: "I saw the ring." Questioned as to how he knew the stone was a sapphire, he replied: "Never mind how I know, I know!"

At this point of the report Captain Macdonald adds a note to the effect that, wishing to leave the house after Voirrey had gone into the stackyard (before Gef screamed) he found the door locked: "The Irvings said: 'That's Gef', but there was no proof that Voirrey herself did not lock the door behind her when she went out."

The Captain had to wait until the girl returned and unfastened the door, before he could leave the house. When Voirrey rejoined them in the living room, it was stated that Gef would do the coin trick for the Captain. It did not transpire how this was arranged; whether Gef promised beforehand that he would do it at a certain time. All the report tells us is that "After this came the demonstration of the coins (head or tail)". Captain Macdonald went into the porch and Irving asked him to place a penny in a certain position on the deep ledge of the window.

Irving says in his report: "You went into the porch, and I showed you where to place a penny, and you were to satisfy yourself that we three (self, wife, and. Voirrey) were so placed in our living room that it would be an absolute impossibility for any of us to see the coin."

This sounds remarkably like a conjuring trick, and it is worth noting that, for the first time during any visit by Captain Macdonald, the entire Irving family was in view while the alleged manifestation by Gef took place. Captain Macdonald placed a penny in the porch and, it is presumed, returned to the room with Irving, though the report is silent on this point.

"The first time Gef named the coin wrongly." We are not told how, or from where, Gef spoke. Then the Captain returned to the porch and Gef called out: "Hanky panky work, he has not touched the coin!"

This was correct, but of course, Gef – or whoever called out – could hear that the coin was not moved or tossed. The Captain then tossed the coin again, and Gef called out correctly. The sum total of this "trick" was that Gef, in two calls, was right once and wrong once – exactly what chance would account for. The interesting part of this story is that if Irving, his wife, and Voirrey were in the presence of Captain Macdonald when Gef made the calls, where did the "voice" come from? The room is dark, whether by day or lamplight, but not so dark but that ventriloquism could have accounted for the voice. We are not told the exact positions of each member of the Irving family, where Captain Macdonald sat, and where the "voice" came from. But there is no evidence whatever that the owner of the "voice" saw the coins: the calls were sheer guess-work.

During the next day (May 21st) Captain Macdonald and Mr. Irving walked about the village of Glen Maye, and had lunch at the Waterfall Hotel. Upon their return to the farm, Mrs. Irving at once told the Captain what their conversation at Glen Maye had been about, and what Irving had had to drink for lunch. She stated that Gef had been present, unseen, during the meal, and had followed them about. The animal reached the farm before her husband and the Captain, and had given Mrs. Irving an account of some of their doings.

Without suggesting that anything of the sort took place, it is obvious that collusion between Mr. and Mrs. Irving could have accounted for the seeming miracle.

Later, when Voirrey was again in the stackyard "feeding the hens", Captain Macdonald and Mr. and Mrs. Irving heard Gef call out: "Plus fours. Oxford bags," an allusion to the way that the Captain was dressed. Mr. Irving continues his report to Captain Macdonald: "When he [Gef] said these words, the voice was a few feet away, and behind the wainscot, my wife and self were both within a few feet from you, and in full view also, and Voirrey at this moment (and this is important) was 100 feet away from the house, out of sight and out of sound in the stackyard; and I at once asked you to come to the window and see for yourself, and in 2 or 3 seconds, she appeared at the entrance to the stackyard, coming towards the house."

Of course, there is no proof whatever that Voirrey was a hundred feet away when the "voice" manifested. All that the Captain saw was the girl returning from somewhere, after the voice had manifested. There is no evidence as to where the girl was when the voice was speaking. It is a pity that Gef again waited until the girl left the house before he spoke.

It was midnight when Captain Macdonald left the farmhouse. Mr. Irving accompanied his guest to the hotel. Mrs. Irving and Voirrey remained in the house. The night was quite dark. When the Captain and his host were eighty paces from the house "Gef called out 'Coo-eel' to us". The animal afterwards admitted that it was he calling out, ten feet from where the two men were walking. But again there is no proof that either Mrs. Irving or Voirrey were where they were supposed to be, viz. in the farmhouse. Mr. Irving concludes his report to Captain Macdonald in the following words: "Now what I wish to impress upon you is this: in these two experiences, you have had what no one else has had (excepting ourselves), that is, you heard him speak in the house whilst my daughter was out of the house (100 feet away), and he spoke to us both, outside the house and when my daughter was in the house."

Unfortunately, there is no real evidence that Voirrey was not out of the house when she was supposed to be in; or in the house when she was supposed to be out. It was a pity that Captain Macdonald did not prepare the report himself.

CHAPTER III

THE INVESTIGATORS AT WORK

MR. IRVING'S report of Captain Macdonald's second visit somewhat perturbed Gef, who demanded that it should be read over to him before being forwarded to London. Irving did so, and the animal remarked: "Captain Macdonald was here and knows it all, so what is the object of your writing it to him?" Irving replied that his friend wished him to write it, to which Gef retorted: "Captain Macdonald will be showing it to Harry Price." He added that he did not mind the Captain seeing it, but Price! Gef's aversion to Mr. Price is significant.

For years previously he had shown signs of fear when any reference to Mr. Price was made in his hearing. "Mr. Price is a doubter!"; "Mr. Price puts the kybosh on the spirits!"; "I don't like Mr. Price"…and so on. But as the case of the "talking mongoose" was originally reported to Mr. Price for his opinion and advice, he decided to turn his attention to the affair and investigate the alleged phenomena. As he required an intelligent and impartial witness to accompany him to Doarlish Cashen, he invited Mr. R. S. Lambert, the Editor of *The Listener*, to co-operate in the inquiry. Mr. Lambert consented.

On June 28th 1935 we wrote to Mr. Irving, saying that we intended visiting the farm sometime during July. We asked the farmer whether there was anything we could bring him. Mr. Irving replied (July 2nd) that he would be glad to see us, but, unfortunately, Gef was missing. The animal had disappeared on the very day that we wrote to say we were coming. But as the mongoose often slipped away for a day or two's holiday, no one was particularly concerned about his absence. Irving gave us the fullest instructions as to reaching the island and his farm. But these were not necessary, as the farmer himself promised to meet the boat at Douglas, and, so that his visitors could be recognized, enclosed a couple of sprigs of white mountain flax which he asked us to wear in our buttonholes. He, too, promised to wear a similar flower, in order that we could identify him. In response to our offer to bring something from London, Mr. Irving said he would like a camera. He also kindly invited us to stay at his little farm-house 'as by doing so there is a good chance of hearing Gef speak himself, if he returns by then'. From this last remark we gathered that Mr. Irving did not expect Gef to return. We did not accept the Irvings' offer to sleep at Doarlish Cashen, as there was no suitable accommodation. We decided to visit the Isle of Man on July 30th 1935.

On July 7th Mr. Irving wrote that Gef was still missing. He added that not since 1932 had the mongoose been absent for so protracted a period, and that probably he was at one of the aerodromes on the island. Gef was definitely interested in flying, and often spent days studying the latest machines. We suggested that perhaps the animal was learning to fly, and would turn up when we arrived, and give us a surprise.

Mr. Irving wrote again on July 19th and reported that Gef was "still missing". He said: "I had, perhaps too hastily, connected his disappearance with your proposed visit to us, but since then, on further consideration, it has occurred to me to ask myself, why should he disappear nearly five weeks before your expected visit?"

Why, indeed? It will be noted that Mr. Irving, on July 19th, did not anticipate Gef returning by July 30th.

The thought occurred to both Mr. Lambert and Mr. Price that it might be advantageous to postpone their visit to the island until Gef returned to the farm. But as Mr. Irving appeared to take it for granted that the mongoose would not be present during our investigation, we decided to adhere to our original plans, especially as the weather was fine and there was a chance of having a smooth passage between Liverpool and Douglas.

We left London on Tuesday, July 30th 1935, and arrived at Douglas at 6:45 the same evening. We were met on the quay by Mr. Irving, easily recognizable by the sprig of mountain flax in his button-hole. The recognition was mutual, and the farmer warmly greeted us. He had a roomy car waiting, and very soon we were speeding towards Glen Maye, the charming beauty-spot about fifteen miles from Douglas. Rooms had been booked for us at the Waterfall Hotel, a comfortable inn at the top of the glen.

After a wash, Mr. Irving accepted our invitation to dinner, and it turned out to be a most interesting meal. For nearly two hours Irving related the complete story of the elusive mongoose; from the time he took up his abode at the farmstead, until he – very unfortunately – disappeared when he learnt of our proposed investigation. Gef was still missing. Over our chops and beer we received a detailed verbal picture of Gef's doings, covering nearly four years. We discovered that Mr. Irving has a very fine memory, as his recital of the scores of incidents in the history of Gef invariably coincided (almost word for word) with what had been recorded in the letters sent to Captain Macdonald and Mr. Price.

GEF'S 'SANCTUM' IN VOIRREY'S ROOM

ON TOP OF WHICH HE TAKES HIS FOOD, DANCES AND BOUNCES HIS
FAVOURITE BALL. NOTE THE CHAIR, WHICH THE 'MONGOOSE' PUSHES
ABOUT BY WAY OF EXERCISE

THE LIVING-ROOM AT DOARLISH CASHEN

SHOWING PANELLING AND DOOR LEADING TO STAIRCASE TO UPPER ROOMS
(CLOUD EFFECT DUE TO MAGNESIUM SMOKE)

Dinner over, we suggested a stroll up the mountain to the haunt of Gef, in order to make a preliminary survey. Mr. Irving said he did not think it would be of much use, and that we had better see the place by daylight. However, he was persuaded to take us up to the farm, and after an hour's stiff climb up a rugged and awkward path, the summit was reached. Just as the house appeared dimly in the failing light (it was practically dark), a minor shock was in store for us. As we approached the house, an animal bounded into our midst; it was Mona, the beautiful brown and black collie sheep-dog, who had heard her master's voice, and had rushed to greet him and his guests. Immediately, Mr. Martin Duncan's judgment that Gef's specimen hairs originated on a collie was recalled by both of the present writers. If only Mona could have spoken!

Mr. Irving led the way to the little farmstead (really a cottage), opened the door, and ushered us through the porch (where Gef does the "penny trick"), and into the living-room, where he introduced us to Mrs. Irving and his daughter, Voirrey. Although Irving had stated during dinner that we were not expected, his wife was apparently waiting for us. We found her to be particularly charming and dignified, with eyes that can best be described as "magnetic": a very striking personality.

She gave us a warm welcome, and asked us to make ourselves at home. We found Voirrey a rather quiet, shy, girl; good looking and intelligent. We gave her the camera which we had purchased for her, and she seemed pleased. We all sat down round the small, dark-panelled living-room, illuminated by a table paraffin lamp whose rays were mostly absorbed by the almost black match-boarding with which the walls of the room were covered. Verbal felicities over, we heard the Gef story once more. By this time we almost knew it by heart. We plied Mrs. Irving and Voirrey with questions about their strange guest (who was still missing) and their answers (Voirrey spoke very little) tallied with what we had learnt from letters to Captain Macdonald and Mr. Irving's own story as related to us at the Waterfall lim. Hardly a detail was omitted.

Mrs. Irving stated that she and her husband were heart-broken at Gef's continued absence of nearly five weeks. Such a thing had never occurred before. As a matter of fact, she was not absolutely certain that the mongoose was missing; she thought that he was somewhere about the place, hiding and voiceless. At that very moment he might have his eye to a squint-hole, taking stock of the intruders who had so ruthlessly invaded his privacy. She was so certain that he was on the premises that, in a voice quivering with emotion, she addressed a pathetic little speech to him in the hope that it would touch a sympathetic chord somewhere and induce him to come out. She argued that we had travelled a long way for the express purpose of hearing him speak, and that it was ungracious of him – to put it mildly – to remain silent. She appealed to his better nature. But there was no response.

Then, Mr. Price tried what he could do. Addressing the four walls of the room, he implored the animal to say a few words. Or, if he preferred, a little laugh, a scream, or just a simple scratch behind the panelling. He invited him to throw something at him – or even spit at him, his favourite way of dealing with "doubters". But Mr. Price's eloquence was quite wasted: not even a squeak was heard. Mrs. Irving was still convinced that the animal was in the house, and gave as one of her arguments that about a fortnight previously a saucepan of water had mysteriously fallen off the stove in the living room, wetting her husband's boots. No one was in the room and she thought that Gef must have been the culprit. We heard a good deal more of the animal's doings – and, especially, sayings – and it was midnight before we decided to climb down the mountain to our hotel. Mr. Irving kindly escorted us, and" with the aid of two electric torches we groped and stumbled our way back to the village, where we said good-bye to our host.

Arrived at the inn, a "council meeting" was held in Mr. Lambert's bedroom, and the whole situation was reviewed and discussed. Was the "mongoose" a myth? Was there any evidence that Gef had ever existed? These and similar questions are discussed elsewhere in this volume. But it seemed incredible that the Irvings could invent and sustain such a story, unless there was some foundation for it. Mrs. Irving's impassioned appeal to Gef to "come out" would have brought tears to the eyes of less hardened investigators than ourselves, and if she were merely playing a part – what a consummate actress! As our speculations merely made us more drowsy, without getting us anywhere, we decided to turn in and sleep on the problem. It was then 2 a.m.

Before we left the Irvings on the previous evening we suggested that Voirrey might like to motor round the island with us. We had decided to spend the morning visiting the Manx beauty-spots, and thought the girl would be pleased to accompany us. She accepted at once, but Mr. Irving said that he would also like to go with us. Actually, we had no intention of inviting him, as we wanted to have a quiet chat with Voirrey away from her parents. We thought that perhaps she could have enlightened us upon several points which Irving had overlooked. As a matter of fact, we had quite a string of questions to put to her privately. But since her father wished to come with us this was impossible.

We therefore spent the morning of Wednesday, July 31st, in motoring round the Isle of Man accompanied by Mr. Irving and

Voirrey. It was the girl's first visit to the north of the island, a fact which struck us as being very extraordinary. Irving chatted most of the way, and, for the third time during our short visit, we heard the complete Gef story with a wealth of detail. Gef was still missing. After lunch we motored to as near Doarlish Cashen as we could get, but found we still had a long uphill walk to reach the farmhouse, where we arrived about four o'clock. It was a glorious afternoon, with the sun beating down on us and making everything look beautiful. St. Patrick's Channel shone like a mirror, and, far below us, Peel had the appearance of a toy town made of children's bricks. The sunlight made the place look even more desolate than it did by night, and there was a curious stillness owing to the absence of living things. An occasional hawk flew high above us, and that was about all.

We received another warm welcome from Mrs. Irving, and found that she had gone to considerable trouble in preparing for us a substantial meal, which was much appreciated. She informed us that Gef was still missing, though she had called him several times. Before we sat down to the high tea which was set for us Mr. Irving showed us all over the house, especially Gef's haunts, some of which we photographed. In the porch we saw an overhead trap-door which gives access to the roof above. We saw the crack through which Gef is alleged to peep during the "penny trick". His line of vision was demonstrated to us by Irving, with the aid of a mirror. Inside a recess portions of the partition wall had been removed in order to provide the animal with a run from porch into house. The principal runs of Gef are between walls and panelling.

He has many squint-holes, especially in the southeast corner of the living-room, where there is a dark recess or shelf over the cupboard where papers, etc., are kept. It is on this shelf that Gef sometimes sits, and it was here that Mrs. Irving saw the animal and felt his teeth. He nipped her and drew blood, afterwards apologizing and advising the use of ointment. We were also shown the slits in ceiling and panels through which he dropped or threw pins, needles, small stones, etc., at "doubters", with exceedingly accurate aim. We saw a knob off a drawer, broken tile, boxwood "men" belonging to an Indian board game, etc., which, at various times, Gef had thrown about. We examined another squint-hole where the animal is supplied with food in the shape of chocolate biscuits, bilberries, and Post Toasties. He refuses milk, or bread and milk. We also inspected the various objects that Gef had 'found' on his wanderings: a pair of gloves, pincers, coins, etc.

Our host conducted us to the upper floor haunts, the principal of which is "Gef's sanctum" in Voirrey's room. This "sanctum" is really the top of the boxed-in staircase. It is on this this that the mongoose spends much of his time (especially at night); takes his food, fires "wise-cracks" at his hosts, bounces his pall, and performs the sarabande to the music of the gramophone.

On this "sanctum" is usually a chair which – perhaps by way of exercise – Gef pushes about, especially when the Irvings want to go to sleep. Beams supporting the roof leave a considerable gap by means of which the mongoose can pass from Voirrey's room to that of her, parents with lightning rapidity. Attempts have been made to block this aperture by means of nails and boards, but all to no purpose: Gef still manages to slip from one room to the other. The fact that the interior of the entire house is panelled with stained match-boarding (there is a space of about three or four inches between wood and wall) provides Gef with as many runs as a rabbit-warren.

Outside the house we saw various "exits and entrances" used by Gef, one of which, in the wall, we reproduce herewith. Irving then showed us a favourite spot in the sod hedge where the mongoose leaves the rabbits which he strangles; this, too, we photographed. We also took pictures of the house itself, the Irving family, and lively Mona.

After tea we again explored the fields and outbuildings round Cashen's Gap, and took more photographs. Mona accompanied us and, acting upon Mr. Martin Duncan's suggestion, we took specimens of Mona's fur. With a pair of nail scissors we clipped pieces from various parts of the collie's coat, for comparison with those alleged to have been plucked by the mongoose out of his own back and tail. Another reason why we left the house was because someone suggested that if we absented ourselves for a short period perhaps Gef (who was still thought to be in hiding) would manifest himself to the Irvings and tell them why he would not speak to us. Mrs. Irving promised to make another appeal on our behalf. But the plan failed. When we returned to the cottage Gef was still missing.

About midnight we decided that it was useless to remain at Cashen's Gap any longer. Gef had had a month's notice of our visit; he had been appealed to 'by the Irvings and by ourselves, but had persisted in absenting himself – to his own very great disadvantage. For if we could have told the world that we had seen – or even heard – the animal he would have gone down to posterity as the most wonderful mongoose that had ever been known. Also he would have made the Irvings a fortune. He lost a literally golden opportunity. Of course our hosts were very sorry that we had to leave the island without that evidence for which we had travelled so far. They said they had done their best, and could not possibly understand why Gef had hidden himself for nearly five weeks. He had never done such a thing before, and they feared that some ill had befallen him. Perhaps the men at the bus depot had knocked him on the head with a spanner, or perhaps he had been run over by a bus.

We told the Irvings that we were even more sorry than they at not seeing their protégé, and did not know what our London friends would say when we returned home. We thanked our hosts for their hospitality, and for the pleasant hours we had spent under their roof. They had done everything for us – except produce Gef! Mr. Irving once more accompanied us down the mountain path to the village. On our way to the inn we thought that perhaps Gef would relent at the last moment and, from behind a sod hedge, squeak a little "coo-eel" by way of a farewell. But we were to experience this final disappointment. Irving's last words to us were an earnest reiteration of the truth of everything that he had told us about Gef.

Next afternoon we left the island, arriving at Liverpool in the early evening. Though we had not seen Gef, our journey was by no means wasted, as we had acquired some valuable information. Incidentally, we had also discovered what the villagers of Glen Maye thought of the mongoose story. We interviewed a number of the inhabitants (Irving's nearest neighbours), but could not find a single person who would vouch for Gef. Everyone knew the story by heart, and some had actually been to Doarlish Cashen in the hope of seeing the "Dalby Spook", the name by which the animal is known locally. We had a long chat with a young farmer who frequently slept at Doarlish Cashen before the Irvings took the place. He neither saw nor heard anything that could be considered abnormal, and did not believe in Gef. He told us the story of a farmer who was looking for his sheep, saw Gef, and took to his heels. This was denied by the man, and it must be admitted that the yarn sounds improbable. We came to the conclusion that Irving's neighbours did not believe in Gef, though a few had acted if they did. They think there is something mysterious connected with Doarlish Cashen, and some are a little afraid.

.   .   .   .   .

As we left the island the mongoose returned to the farm house; in fact, we must have passed him on the r o a d to the coast. In a letter (August 6th) Mr. Irving told us that on the previous Thursday (the day we left for the mainland), at midnight, it threw some object into their bedroom. "He clapped his hands and laughed like a maniac." No one answered him at first as the Irvings were "much too angry and mortified that he had let us down". His first words were: "Well, I've come back!" Mrs. Irving replied: "Nobody wants you here; you should have stayed away." He said he had been all over the island. He was asked: "Were you in when Mr. Harry Price and Mr. Lambert were here?" Gef answered: "I should just think I was!" He said he did not speak because there was a "doubter' present, in the person of Mr. Lambert. He said nothing about his previous antipathy to Mr. Price. He accurately described both of the present writers, saying that Mr. Price was wearing a signet ring on which was a crest. "He looked like a minister," concluded Gef, who admitted that it was he who had knocked over the saucepan of water in the living room. As some amends for his absence during our visit, Gef promised Irving that he would make imprints of his paws, which could be sent to us. The farmer therefore asked us to send him some plasticine.

After we had returned to London, Voirrey became very active with the camera that we had presented to her for the purpose of photographing Gef. She made several attempts, and forwarded the results to us for our inspection. It must be candidly admitted that it required a good deal of imagination to recognize in the photographs any sort of animal. In one or two pictures "Gef" looked like a piece of rock stuck on top of a sod hedge; in others, nothing animalish was visible. Voirrey was asked to try again, and more spools were sent for this purpose.

Finally she produced something that might be recognized as an animal, but discussion of this photograph may appropriately be left to a later chapter in this book. We also asked Irving if he could not get the mongoose to sit on his knees, and then ask Voirrey to photograph it; but apparently this was not possible. We have done the best we could in the way of photographs, but the reader must be content with the picture of the animal which was drawn from the precise details given us by Irving and Gef!

A pound of plasticine was soon sent to Mr. Irving for the express purpose of obtaining Gef's paw prints. Gef tried it and said it was too hard. The farmer then softened it with Vaseline and the mongoose made another attempt. This was more successful. The modelling clay was placed o n top of his "sanctum" and Gef stuck his hind foot in it. He did this while the Irvings were asleep and they found the paw print in the morning. It was immediately dispatched to London. Gef was asked how he managed it. He said: "I put my foot in it, and gave it a twist, but the stuff was as hard as hell!" On August 19th we received further imprints of Gef's paws. They are extremely interesting; the more so as the three specimens differ from one another. Apparently, Gef has different kinds of paws. It would be interesting to know what the other two are like. In the photograph which we reproduce, A is an imprint in dough, and represents Gef's right "hand", with extended "fingers". B is a plasticine impression of the same "hand" with "fingers" in their normal position. C is an imprint of a hind foot, and D are teeth marks (two sets) made by the animal biting into a piece of plasticine with his top teeth. He was asked how he made these impressions in the plasticine, etc., which had been left on his "sanctum" when the Irvings went to bed. At 6.30 the following morning, when Irving was lying in bed awake, Gef had a sly peep at his benefactor and gave a long-drawn-out call of "Ji . . . m!" Irving asked if he had made the impressions. Gef replied: "Go and find out!" From the tone of his voice the farmer knew that the prints had been made. Later, he asked the mongoose whether the teeth marks were those of the top or bottom jaw. Gef said: "Top jaw." He was then asked how he managed to avoid the impress of his lower jaw, if he bit the plasticine. Gef replied: "I did not put it in my mouth like a piece of bread; I put my teeth down on it." So now the reader knows the history of the teeth impressions. Immediately on receipt of these very interesting exhibits, we photographed them and afterwards sent a print to the distinguished zoologist, Mr. R. I. Pocock, F.R.S., Temporary Assistant in the Zoological Department of the British Museum since 1923. Mr. Pocock, in a letter, gave his opinion concerning the alleged paw prints:

BRITISH MUSEUM (NATURAL HISTORY), CROMWELL ROAD, LONDON, S.W.7 .

5th October 1935

DEAR SIR,

A. This does not represent the foot print of any mammal known to me, except possibly a raccoon, an American animal.

B. Has no connection with A. Conceivably it was made by a dog. There is no other British mammal that could have done it.

C. Has no possible connection with B. There is no mammal in which there is such a disparity in the size of the fore and hind foot.

D. This does not appear to me to represent tooth marks. Finally I must add that I do not believe these photographs represent foot tracks at all. Most certainly none of them was made by a mongoose.

Very truly yours, (Signed) R. I. POCOCK

So the reader will note that instead of elucidating the mystery, Gef's "paw prints" merely increased it. According to expert opinion, we now know that Gef's "right hand" might be the foot of a raccoon; the same hand closed may be that of a dog; his hind foot has no connection with his forefoot, whether open or closed; that very probably they are not paw prints at all; but if they are, they were not made by a mongoose. Is it a no wonder that the Gef mystery is so intriguing?

The reader will remember that during our visit to Doarlish Cashen, we clipped some portions of fur from various parts of Mona's anatomy. We sent them to Mr. Martin Duncan, who again very kindly devoted much time and skill to identifying them. The authors would like to take this opportunity of publicly thanking him for his assistance in their inquiry. His evidence is vital. Mr. Duncan quickly discovered that the specimens of fur alleged to have grown on Gef, actually grew on Mona, the Irvings' collie sheepdog. In a letter dated August 13th, 1935 he says:

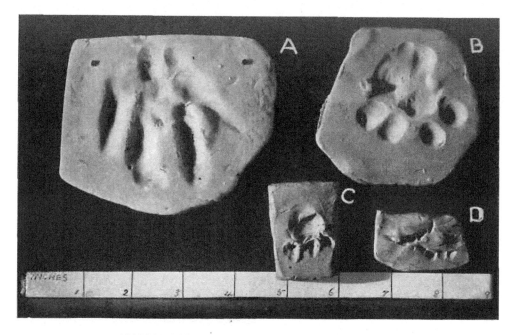

ALLEGED FOOT TRACKS AND TEETH MARKS OF GEF

A—right fore paw with 'fingers' extended

B—right fore paw with 'fingers' in normal position

C—hind paw

D—teeth marks (upper jaw, two sets)

A represents an impression in dough; the remainder are imprints in plasticine

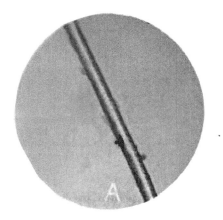

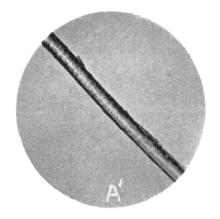

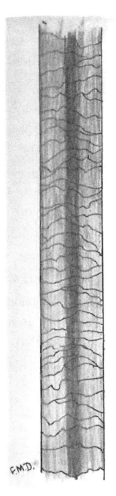

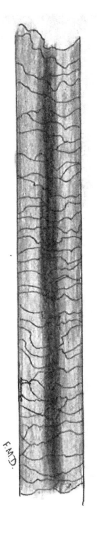

A—Photomicrograph of fine hair of Gef's undercoat

A[1]—Photomicrograph of fine hair of undercoat of Red Setter
Magnified × 350

B—Hair from second sample 'Talking Mongoose'

B[1]—Hair from Collie Dog Mona
Magnified × 500

Photomicrographs and camera-lucida drawings by F. Martin Duncan, F.Z.S.

GEF THE TALKING MONGOOSE

ZOOLOGICAL GARDENS, REGENT's PARK, LONDON, N.W.8

DEAR MR. PRICE,

Many thanks for your letter of August 8th, with samples of hairs from the 'talking mongoose', and the sample from the collie sheep-dog 'Mona' which you had been able yourself to collect.

As I expected, your sample on examination is absolutely identical with the alleged 'mongoose' hairs. I have made four camera-Lucida drawings, all x 500: one from the first sample you received; one from the second sample which included the vibrisae; and two from two hairs from 'Mona' which you had collected . . . . They clearly demonstrate that they all came from the same animal – the dog – and not from any 'mongoose'. I return the hair samples along with the drawings, which I hope · will be of some help to you.

Yours sincerely,

(Signed) F. MARTIN DUNCAN

So what are we to think of Gef's story that he pulled the samples of fur out of his own back, etc.? A glance at Mr. Duncan's drawings will convince the most credulous that all the fur we received in London originated on Mona. The reader is faced with alternative solutions to the mystery: (A) That some person robbed Mona of portions of her fur, with the idea of providing 'evidence' for the mongoose story; or (B) that Gef clipped bits of fur off Mona and foisted them on the Irvings as specimens of his own hirsute covering.

After the investigators returned to London, various references to them were made by Gef. During a heart-to-heart talk (which lasted one and a half hours) to Irving on August 10th, the mongoose was asked why he did not talk during our visit. He laughed "not unpleasantly", used some rather strong language, and said: "I know something!". Irving replied: "Well, what is it? Out with it!" Gef answered: "When Mr. Harry Price and Mr. Lambert were standing somewhere near the cart-shed, Mr. Lambert said: "It would be more satisfactory if Gef spoke, if there were no one in the house." This alleged remark of Gef refers to the period of our visit when we were wandering round the outbuildings after tea at the farm. As a matter of fact, Gef's story is pure fiction. Of course we were talking about Gef, but it never occurred to us that we should like to hear him when the Irving family was out of the house. We would have much preferred the mongoose to speak to us when all the Irvings were in the same room, under close observation. As Gef is so clever at eavesdropping, why did he not hear our conversation when we were clipping pieces off Mona on the far side of a barn? Because that is when Mr. Lambert's remark was supposed to have been made. And I am afraid we cannot credit Gef with "X-ray eyes", or he would have seen what was going on behind the barn.

It has been stated more than once in these pages that Mr. Irving is singularly consistent in his oft-repeated and detailed history of Gef. What he wrote to Captain Macdonald corresponds in almost every particular with what he related to us; and the answers to the string of questions with which we cross-examined him invariably tallied with what he said in his letters to the Captain. It is all the more surprising, then, that there should be a curious discrepancy in the first two letters we received after our return from the Isle of Man. It will be remembered that we left the island on Thursday, August 1st. On Friday, August 2nd, Mr. Irving wrote us to the effect that if we would send him some plastic clay, "I will see if I can obtain Gef's impress of his hands, and also of his feet, *if he returns*... (our italics). In his next letter, dated August 6th, he tells us: "Gef has returned . . . . Late at night, midnight in fact, on *Thurs.* he threw some object into our bedroom. . . .' Thursday was August 1st, the day we left the island. We thought that perhaps "Thurs." was a slip of the pen for "Friday". But in a further letter, dated August 11th, he again refers to Gef as being away from the farm "from June 28th until Aug. 1st", thus confirming the fact that the mongoose *did* return on August 1st. In other words, Irving had been talking to the mongoose several hours before he wrote the words "if he returns".

A few days after our visit to Cashen's Gap, Gef confessed that when we took the flashlight photograph of his "sanctum" in Voirrey's room he was actually upstairs within three or four feet of our camera and magnesium lamp. He said he was behind the panelling and that he "did not like that camera, I was afraid he might take me through the boards" – thinking we had X-ray apparatus. He said he saw the flash through a crack in the match-boarding.

When we returned from our investigation it occurred to us that Voirrey might like to spend a few days in London, and that the holiday would do her good – especially as she has never been nearer the Metropolis than Liverpool. We accordingly wrote to Mr. Irving and suggested his daughter's staying with a lady who was interested in the Gef romance. We promised to meet Voirrey, give her a good time, and put her on the Liverpool train at the end of her holiday. But her parents would not consent, as they considered her "rather young to go so far afield". She is nearly eighteen years of age.

Owing to the great public interest in the "haunting of Cashen's Gap", Mr. Price wrote an account of our investigation which' was published in *The Listener* for September 11th 1935. The article was widely discussed and a number of persons wrote to the journal. Certain people declared that Gef was a myth, and gave their reasons for thinking so. Others made fun of the affair. One of the latter was Mr. J. Radcliffe, a director of the *Isle of Man Examiner*. In a letter to the Editor of *The Listener* (October 23rd 1935), he says:

"I was very surprised to learn that 'Gef' still performs, as, having heard nothing of the 'spook' story since the winter of 1932, I had assumed that 'Gef' had died a natural death. The story in the beginning created a considerable stir in the Isle of Man, and my own experiences are well worth recording. In company with my father (Managing Director of this *Journal*) and a few friends we journeyed to Mr. Irving's cottage one glorious Sunday afternoon, with keen anticipation. Our reception was most cordial, and the subsequent tale unfolded was very similar to your own experience. Despite our coaxing, however, Gef refused to reveal himself or speak up. Somewhat disappointed the party left, and a Mr. Evans and I lingered on the Irving doorstep for a few minutes chatting to Mr. Irving. Suddenly there was a shrill squeak from the corner of the room where Voirrey, the daughter, was sitting, and Mr. Irving in great excitement gripped my arm and pointing to the 'opposite' side of the room whispered: 'He's there! Did you hear him?' Evans and I gazed at each other in sheer amazement. Mr. Irving then suggested that we leave a few coins on the table to see if Gef would come down for them. We were again conducted to the door and the squeaks at intermittent intervals continued. Each squeak was kindly translated by Mr. Irving to mean: 'They don't believe' or 'I want to back a horse', etc. The squeak in every case was of particularly short duration. Mr. Irving decided to accompany us part of the way down that beautiful footpath and invited Voirrey to join us. On our way down I noticed she had a tendency to hang behind, and once again we heard a piping squeak with Mr. Irving again wildly gesticulating and pointing to the hedge (about 2 feet in height) and whispering: 'He's there, I tell you. He's there.' This was really too much, for my hearing is very good, and the squeak without doubt was human and came from immediately behind us. We laughed over the whole incident for days. I say laughed, because it was so badly done that it was extremely funny."

Mr. Radcliffe's negative testimony was balanced by the positive counter-evidence of another gentleman, a Mr. Northwood of Liverpool, who wrote to Mr. Lambert, saying that he knew the Irvings well and that they were honest, reliable, and straightforward people. Not only was he quite convinced of the existence of Gef, but he had actually heard him, and had taken careful notes of the manifestations while they were being produced. He had heard the thumping on the panelling, and had listened to the "voice". This was in 1932. As an expression of good faith, Mr. Northwood enclosed his original notes; the substance of which we reproduce, herewith. We particularly wish to present to our readers every particle of independent, positive evidence for the existence of the 'talking mongoose'.

MR. CHARLES NORTHWOOD'S REPORT

"In October 1931 I saw a statement in the *Daily Dispatch*, and again in the *Daily Mail*, about a talking 'weasel', and noted with astonishment that these revelations occurred at my old friend's home, James Irving of the Isle of Man. I wrote James and he told me all about it as described in *The Listener* about Gef's imitating animals at the outset and later the singing of hymns and nursery rhymes, etc. I had occasion to visit the Isle of Man (March 1932) on certain business and have had close interests there for many years, having married a Manx woman there and three of my five children being christened there. I have great affection for the Island and have visited it yearly for almost 40 years. I arrived there on March 5th 1932 and saw a brother-in-law, Mr. T.; a prominent advocate in Douglas, and had a chat with him over various matters, and he suggested that we drive up to Glen Maye, where Irving lives (whom he knew), and get to know something further about the 'animal'.

"On the next day (Sunday) Mr. T. drove me up there. Mr. T. distinctly told me he 'couldn't believe in an animal talking, it was impossible.' We got to the house. It was a Sunday, and Irving told us all about it and endeavoured to get the 'animal' to speak, but we heard nothing at all. Irving suggested that I go alone. T. didn't believe, and that might be an obstacle, and Gef wouldn't talk before 'doubters'. I said I would come next day. As I have phlebitis in my legs I got a motor-car at Peel and met Mr. Irving at Glen Maye as prearranged, and then drove round the coast road so that I could get to Irving's place without mounting that terrible hill road which could be a big strain on my legs. We therefore walked across the flat and rather marshy land – a sort of plateau – from the coast road. Irving then told me that he had spoken to the animal after T. and I had left the previous day, and he was full of talk. Irving spoke to him and told him of business connections I had at that time in New York, whom Irving also knew, and he spoke to the animal of various details of this business and also about me, with the result that the 'animal' had promised to talk to me.

"He said Gef had mentioned that I had visited the place two years ago with a 'black' fellow that he said was 'a bad man.' He was sure Gef must have been about the place back then. As a matter of fact, I had taken over a fellow out of work to give him a holiday in the Isle of Man, and visited Irving's house with this chap, and later I did find this chap unscrupulous!

"I had taken with me a diary and a lot of foolscap for Irving in order that he should keep a record of this incredible business, as I considered he ought to write a book on it. I also took a parcel of groceries for him. I also was determined to keep a record of anything that was said whilst in the house.

"We arrived at Irving's residence at 12:10 of March 7th 1932. I had been in the house but a few minutes when a telegraph-boy arrived with a telegram for me from my office in Liverpool. I opened it and it was a request that I telephone from Peel (the nearest post office) to Liverpool. I considered this could wait, however, about a minute after this I heard a sort of screech, and Irving turned round to the telegraph-boy and said: 'There you are; that's the animal. Did you hear it?' The boy seemed rather scared, and said he did. Apparently from what Irving told me all the people in Peel are sceptical, especially those in the post office, and this had annoyed Irving. I then sat down and asked Irving for the diary and a couple of sheets of foolscap, and took my watch out and placed it on the table.

"Irving then spoke and said: 'Come on, Gef. Mr. Northwood's here. You promised to speak, you know.' He seemed to treat it just like a child. He then asked me what I would like for lunch. Would I like some bull's heart? I said I didn't mind, and he then asked his daughter ~ prepare lunch. Voirrey went in the back kitchen, and then I distinctly heard in a mild voice: 'Go away, Voirrey', repeated twice from the back kitchen. Irving said: 'Did you hear it, Charlie?' I replied I did.

"Two minutes later (12:17) I heard a high-pitched voice, louder in tone than the last time, say: 'H— B—.' At 12.19: 'How's H— B—?' (This is the American connection spoken of by Irving.) I replied: 'Oh, he's all right the last I heard of him.' Irving then asked him to bark, and he did.

"Irving then asked him to sing 'Carolina Moon', and put the gramophone on with this record. But I heard no singing.

"12:37. Irving trying to get it to speak Hebrew and German, of which he has a smattering. We were then having lunch.

"12:40. I heard from behind the boards in the kitchen: 'Charlie, Charlie, chuck, chuck,,' chuck!' and again: 'Charlie, my old sport!'

"12:45. In a rather loud voice: 'Clear to the devil if you don't believe. Vanished.'

"12.53. Irving asked about the engine driver. (Gef seems fond of this chap, so Irving says.) The animal said: 'What did Jerry Small say to you?' 'He didn't say anything,' replied Irving. 'I just waved my hand to him.' This was the driver of the steam-roller whom we had passed on the road.

"Irving was then trying to get the animal to sing 'Carolina Moon', and again put the gramophone on. 'Does Charlie know it?' says the animal. 'No,' I replied, 'I don't. First I heard of the song was yesterday.' About this time there was a lapse, as I wanted to speak to Irving about other personal matters; so Irving and I talked of various things, Liverpool matters, etc. My time was limited. However Irving was positively itching to get the animal to talk, and said: 'Arthur's coming.' (This was in reference to a young son, aged 20, I had requested to cross over that afternoon and stay overnight at Irving's in order to substantiate further

Irving's statements.) 'Who's Arthur?' said Gef from behind the boards in the kitchen. 'Mr. Northwood's son,' said Irving. 'He is on the boat.' 'Tell Arthur not to come. He doesn't believe. I won't speak if he does come; I'll blow his brains out with a 3d. cartridge.' Very loud and clear.

"Then heavy thumping on the ceiling and behind the boards in the kitchen as much as a strong man could do. Squeals, and then Gef said: 'Vanished.'

"This was evidently a response to Irving's request to Gef to do his magic. Irving asked the animal: 'What did the Rabbi say?' (Hebrew Rabbi Hillel.) '*Veyho hefto ley macho chomocho*' ('Love thy neighbour as thyself'). Now, Irving had previously mentioned to me in the car whilst we drove from Glen Maye that Gef said Voirrey must stay at home and not go to school, and that he must order a rooster from Simon Hunter and Co. and that it would cost him between 8*s. 6d.* and 15*.S. 6d.* I then heard Gef say: 'Simon Hunter. Have you ordered that rooster, James, from Simon Hunter? Mind you do so. Have you posted that letter?' 'Yes,' said Irving, and handed me the letter to read, and Irving said: 'Here, you read it out, Charlie.' So I read the letter out to the animal. I then heard a slight squeal later.

"A little after this from behind the boards in the sitting-room, possibly some 25-30 feet away, I heard a very loud voice penetrating and with some malice in it: '*You don't believe. You are a doubter*', etc.'

"This was very startling, and for the first time put a bit of a shiver through me. Equal to a couple of irascible women's voices put together!

"I said: 'I do believe.' I had to shout this. A little later, at 3 p.m., came a voice from the porch: 'Charlie.' Very loud and clear, and appeared quite close.

At 3.5 a voice: 'Is Arthur coming?' This in the kitchen. A screech, and then a loud thump the other end of the house.

"At 3 p.m. I got another telegram from my office in Liverpool that I must go to the phone at Peel and telephone to Liverpool. Irving offered to accompany me down the hill, which I didn't mind, and his daughter also came. About three-quarters of the way down this road I heard a screech from behind the hedge. Irving turned to me and said: 'Did you hear him?' I said: 'Yes.'

"About another 100 yards farther on another screech, and about another 100 yards more and again another screech. Evidently he had followed us down! We were then close on Glen Maye, and reached the Waterfall Hotel at 3.40 p.m. and I then got in the waiting motor-car and went on to Peel."

·　　·　　·　　·　　·

Mr. Northwood's report is impressive, but an analysis will show that he nowhere makes the statement that Mr. Irving and Voirrey Irving were both in his immediate presence when the "voice" was heard. Mrs. Irving, says Mr. Northwood, was away from home at the time.

Mr. Northwood very kindly gave us an interview on October 14th 1935, when he confirmed the statements made in his report. A resume of our discussion appears as Appendix C. Subsequently Mr. Northwood's son Arthur, who is in the Royal Artillery, wrote to Mr.

Lambert confirming what his father had told us, and also averring his own belief in the reality of Gef.

One of the persons most interested in our visit to Doarlish Cashen was Captain Macdonald. It will be remembered that he visited the Isle of Man in February 1932 and May 1935, in an endeavour to clear up the Gef mystery. He was not successful. Not only did our failure to hear or see the mongoose in July 1935 surprise him, but he was disappointed that we could not prove the existence of the animal. He therefore decided to pay a third visit to the island. He arrived at Doarlish Cashen on October 2nd 1935, and afterwards wrote up his adventures. Fortunately, on this occasion he prepared the report himself, and the following is the verbatim copy:

REPORT OF CAPTAIN MACDONALD'S THIRD VISIT

"I arrived with Mr. Irving at Doarlish Cashen, Isle of Man, at approximately 5:30 p.m., Tuesday afternoon, October 2nd 1935. Mrs. Irving and her daughter Voirrey greeted me, and the former said that Gef had been in the house practically all day, talking and shouting at the top of his voice. I inquired if Mrs. Irving thought that Gef was still there; she replied that he told her that he was going down to the Waterfall Inn to see us arrive there, so that she did not think that he was back yet, although Gef said that he was returning to have a good talk to me and, if possible, give me a lively night.

"I sat with the family in the kitchen (sitting- room), hoping that Gef would return at any moment, but no sign of him at all, and at 9 p.m. I really began to think that he did not mean to return at all.

"However, at 9.30 p.m., we all heard the geese (these are the only birds not shut in at night) making a clucking noise (i.e. noise of alarm), and the family at once said they must have seen Gef on his way in. I ascertained that these birds often herald the approach of Gef.

"We waited patiently, expecting to hear Gef at any moment, but although Mr. and Mrs. Irving kept calling him, there was blank silence. As it was getting late, Mrs. Irving told Voirrey (the daughter) to go to bed, and this she did, and at 11 p.m. Mr. Irving and myself went up to her room and saw that she was in bed.

"We (Mr. Irving and self) then returned to the kitchen. I should mention that Mr. and Mrs. Irving sleep over the kitchen, and Voirrey's room is opposite on the other side of the staircase.

"At 11:30 p.m. we three (Mr. and Mrs. Irving and self) suddenly heard a few raps, and Mr. Irving shouted: 'Is that you, Gef?' To this there was: no reply, so I shouted: 'Come on, Gef; if you won't talk, make a noise.' In response to this request, raps of various qualities of sound started from different points of the house with great rapidity. I then heard a bedroom door banged with extraordinary violence, so suggested we might go upstairs to see what had happened. At that minute a shrill, very excited, and highly pitched voice screamed out: 'Go and look', so up we went and found the fastener on the outside of Voirrey's door was turned down so that she could not get out of the room. (This door I proved could not possibly be fastened from the inside-it must be done from the outside, as it is merely a turn-button fixed by a screw on the outside of the door.) We again saw Voirrey in bed, and she said Gef was overhead, between the slate roof and ceiling. Before leaving the bedroom, I asked Mr. Irving to fasten me in, in order to satisfy myself that it was impossible to get out without smashing the door down. I found that I was unable to get out until released from the outside. Before leaving the door, I again fastened it, and we both again returned to the kitchen, and sat near the fire to await further events.

"The voice then started in earnest, and the noise in the house was amazing. Shrill screams accompanied by terrific knocking, loud bangs, emanated from all parts of the house in quick succession (as if the perpetrator moved with lightning speed). The bangs appeared to come from the roof, Mr. and Mrs. Irving's room over the kitchen, and on the staircase. The noise continued for about 15 minutes, culminating with tremendous bangs as if something had been thrown with violence upstairs. So upstairs we went again to Voirrey's room, unfastened the door, and found her in bed. I flashed my lamp round the room, and found that a heavy chair which Mrs. Irving had put on the staircase covering, had been flung from its place and fallen partly on the bed and partly on to a chest of drawers. Voirrey, who was awake, said: 'Oh, it's only some more of Gef's tricks', but did not appear at all perturbed.

"Before descending, I again fastened the door, and we returned to the kitchen. The voice began again louder than ever, so I asked that it might come quite close so that I could hear all that was being said. The voice said: 'Listen, I will imitate a steam-whistle.' So we then had a demonstration of this – the note was very clear and of wonderful timbre. I then shouted: 'Gef, wait a minute and I will time you doing the whistle.' I then counted '1, 2, 3, off!' Away went the voice, but 22 seconds was the duration of time.

"I then said: 'Gef, that's enough of the whistle; now come down close to us here, as I'm tired of shouting at you.' Within a few seconds there was a very loud bang on the lower part of the staircase panelling, which nearly shook the pictures off their hooks, as all were oscillating. I shouted: 'That's splendid, Gef, knock the blinking house down!' To this he laughed loudly, so I said: 'Gef, let's have one of your demoniacal laughs,' but although we had it, my blood did not freeze in my veins! I then said: 'Do come much nearer to us', and hardly had I finished speaking, when the voice came practically to the kitchen entrance and shouted: 'Hello, everybody!' This occurred two or three times, and on the two latter occasions I rushed out with my flash-lamp, threw a beam of light up the staircase, only to find no one there, ·but to be greeted with a shout away in the distance: 'You damned sleech' (Manx for sly man).

"As I was returning down the staircase and just entering the kitchen, a bottle and a china tray were flung from the top of the staircase – the latter being smashed in the fall – this was accompanied by a derisive laugh. I again examined Voirrey's door – it was fastened. The voice then said: 'Spies.' We asked what that meant, and it replied: 'Someone outside the house poaching your rabbits.' Mr. Irving and self went out and thought we heard someone, but could not be sure. On: returning, the voice I said: 'I am going. Vanished.' But I asked for more noise, and, to finish with, that the voice might come behind the kitchen panelling. After many arguments, such as: 'You are moving again from your seat', etc., etc., we had a terrific repetition of knocks and bangs all over the house, up and downstairs, and close to us in the panelling, finishing With a shout just behind Mrs. Irving, who was sitting close to the back panelling of the kitchen.

"As it was 3 a.m. we decided to finish, so I said: 'Go and vanish, Gef, to which the voice replied: 'I mean to throw a brick at you tonight when you are asleep.' (I had a little room on the ground floor opposite the kitchen.) The voice then said, 'I'll throw pebbles now at the windows', and almost at once we heard the rattle against them, just as if gravel and sand and small stones were being hurled at them. Mrs. Irving got rather perturbed, and Mrs. Irving told Gef to stop, as she did not want the windows to be broken. I lay on the couch in my room and heard no more until 7 a.m. Thursday, when a voice from near the roof shouted: 'Get up, Macdonald!'

"Owing to the very bad weather and torrential rain, I did not return the next evening. The path up the mountain was almost impassable, the narrow road being like a river, and there were no facilities to dry my clothes; so I left the Island.

(Signed) M. A. MACDONALD

An analysis of Captain Macdonald's report will show that the manifestations did not commence until Voirrey had been sent to bed. As the girl was awake during the whole 'phenomena' period, it was a pity that she was not with her parents and the Captain in the living-room. The report would have been much more impressive if the four of them had been in one room during the whole of the screaming and thumping. And again: emphasis is laid upon the fact that Voirrey was locked in her room during the period when Gef was performing.

It is stressed that the latch outside her room could not be operated from the inside, by the girl herself. But we have no proof of that. With a knife-blade, a needle, or something similar, it *might* be possible to open Voirrey's door from the inside. We are not accusing Voirrey or any member of the Irving family of playing jokes or producing 'phenomena': we are merely criticizing the conditions under which Gef was heard. Instead of locking Voirrey in her room, how much better it would have been to have had the girl under constant observation with the rest of the family.

The chair which usually reposes on what Captain Macdonald rightly calls the 'staircase covering', and which the reader recognizes as "Gef's sanctum" (the identical chair can be seen in our photograph) "had been flung from its place and fallen partly on the (Voirrey's) bed and partly on to a chest of drawers". When they went upstairs to see what the noise was, Voirrey merely said: "Oh, it's only some more of Gef's tricks", and "did not appear at all perturbed". An ordinary girl would have been frightened out of her life if an animal of any description had flung a heavy chair at her while she was in bed. Her composure was as remarkable as Gef's talking. And in what room were the bottle and tray that were thrown downstairs? During his visit to the Isle of Man, Captain Macdonald purchased a bag of cream cakes for Gef, knowing his fondness for them. The bag was put on the top of Gef's "sanctum" in Voirrey's room. After the Captain's departure for the mainland, about 10 o'clock the same evening, Gef put in an appearance, announcing himself by giving a terrific crack on the panelling with his fist. He said: "Has Macdonald gone home?" Mr. Irving said he had, whereupon the mongoose was heard to take a cake out of the bag, and eat it. During the night he ate another cream cake and some ham. Later, he said: "Do you like Macdonald?" Mrs. Irving answered: "Certainly I do; he believes in you." Mr. Irving then asked Gef where he was when he spoke to the Captain on the stairs. He replied: "Part of the time I was on the second from the top, and afterwards I was on the second step from the bottom. I was there when Captain Macdonald hurried to bottom of stairs with the flashlight. I flew upstairs like hell, forgot Voirrey's door was fastened and I banged into it. I had to jump into your room. He nearly saw me!"

Gef was also asked where he was when he spoke to the Captain behind the panelling in the kitchen. He answered: "I was behind the boards where the water comes through."

Mr. Irving explained that this spot is in the comer by the door leading to the pantry. The reader is now acquainted with the history of the "talking mongoose" during his "haunting" of Cashen's Gap, and is in possession of all the facts that we have been able to collect. It remains for us to sum up the case and to suggest certain alternatives to the assertion that Gef is a super-normal animal; or, in fact, an animal at all.

Jim Irving pointing to what could be Gef's fingers protruding along the edge of one of his hiding spots.

CHAPTER IV

WEIGHING UP THE EVIDENCE

ANY attempt to assess the value and analyse the meaning of the events narrated in the foregoing chapters must begin with some consideration of the nature of the evidence. Our main source of knowledge is Irving himself, who, in his letters, diaries and conversation provides us with a copious mass of information concerning Gef which extends over the four years 1932-1935. This information is supplemented and endorsed by the other members of his household vigorously and earnestly in the case of Mrs. Irving, less enthusiastically but equally definitely in the case of Voirrey. In the main, all this testimony of the Irving family agrees well together; it is, in fact, more consistent than might be expected, considering how often eyewitnesses honestly differ from one another in the impressions they receive. Now, these three are, of course, the only persons whose direct testimony is available, that they have both heard, seen, and (in the case of Mrs. Irving) touched the mysterious and elusive Gef. To be sure, Irving tells us that there are some six or seven other persons, living apparently in Peel or Glen Maye, who have either seen or heard Gef at various times and are prepared to admit it – besides others, mainly neighbours, who have seen or heard Gef but are too frightened of ridicule to admit it. But in neither of these cases have we been able to follow up the suggested testimony of these persons, and their evidence cannot therefore be allowed to count.

GEF THE TALKING MONGOOSE

On a different footing, however, is the evidence of Captain Macdonald, who, in his capacity as representing the National Laboratory of Psychical Research, has produced the three written reports previously referred to-one of his first visit in February 1932; the next of his second visit in May 1935; the third of his third visit in October 1935; all of them describing experiences which convinced him that "something was really there". Captain Macdonald apparently both heard and conversed with Gef. We have already noted that the report of his second visit was in the first place put into words for him by Irving himself; nevertheless, Captain Macdonald accepted this report and added his own confirmatory comments. In addition to Captain Macdonald, we have also Irving's friend Mr. Northwood, who gives us a detailed account of his visit to Doarlish Cashen in March 1932, when he heard sufficient of Gef to convince him of the reality of the "talking mongoose" – a conviction he has held firmly ever since. His son, who is now in the Army, accompanied him on this visit, and confirms his father's experiences and conviction.

Finally, we ourselves, visiting Doarlish Cashen subsequently to Captain Macdonald's second visit, neither saw nor heard Gef, but obtained additions to the indirect evidence concerning him, partly by questioning Irving and his family, partly by scrutinizing the farm and its neighbourhood, and partly by carrying off, or afterwards receiving, from Irving material tokens of Gef's person and actions. It is not often that a greater body of evidence is accumulated concerning a so-called supernatural phenomenon. There is, however, some negative testimony to set off against this. Not all the members of the Irving family believe in Gef's existence – Irving's son, as well as his married daughter Elsie, are said to be sceptical. Furthermore, the population of Glen Maye is generally unbelieving: and we have the opinion of the director of the *Isle of Man Examiner* that the occurrences experienced by him in 1932 were susceptible of a natural explanation.

Lastly, however generally consistent the account of Gef given by the Irving family may be, there remain one or two particular inconsistencies which are not easy to explain away. These can perhaps be ascribed to lapses of memory, or to mistakes natural in relation to such a freakish personality as Gef's.

When we proceed to examine the evidence, we find that there are only three possible conclusions to be drawn from it. These are:

(1) That Gef exists and haunts Doarlish Cashen, substantially as the Irvings say he does.

(2) That Gef is a product of hallucination, or fantasy.

(3) That Gef is a product of conscious deception. Acceptance of the first conclusion rules out the other two; but the second and third conclusions are not exclusive of each other, and may be entertained together or separately.

Let us examine the evidence for Gef's existence. The Irvings were of course the first people to become aware of his existence in the autumn of 1931, the hauntings being apparently then confined to the upper story of Doarlish Cashen. According to Irving's letter of November 1th 1934, "We have all three seen him, both before he ever spoke to us, and of course afterwards, at different times." This suggests that Gef was seen before he was heard; but if so these earliest appearances must have been fleeting and unsatisfactory, for as late as June 7th 1932 Irving was writing: "On April 30th he was persuaded to run on the cross-beams which support the roof ... and as we had a fair view, we are able to give a little more detail as to his appearance."

It must be remembered that Gef usually manifests himself late at night, and that the Irving's house is lit only by a modest paraffin lamp. To reconcile the above apparent discrepancies, we must suppose that Gef was first glimpsed indistinctly somewhere on the roof-beams during the autumn of 1931 – before he had learned from Irving to articulate clearly or to converse in English. Since Gef, as late as December 1932, had a great aversion to being seen by Irving, and was also more nervous of Voirrey's movements than of those of her father or mother, it is reason able to infer that Mrs. Irving was the first of the trio to see the strange creature.

Gradually Gef was persuaded to reveal himself more and more distinctly, allowing himself to be fed and touched, until at length he began to be seen downstairs and out of doors, as well as in daylight. At no time have the Irving family varied much in their positive description of Gef's appearance.

"We have all three seen him," says Irving, "in different places and under varying conditions, both indoors and out of doors, in the immediate vicinity of the house, and as far away as Glen Maye village. We have seen him in daylight in the house and also by artificial light, and of course when we saw him out of doors it was broad daylight. My wife and Voirrey have both seen Gef profile and full face. Myself I have seen profile only, not full face. My wife and Voirrey are both agreed that the face is apparently flat. Voirrey, who has had many views, states the nose is flattened at the end, something like a domestic pig's nose; and it was this last-named description of the flat nose which I furnished to the local Press, that brought forth a letter from a retired sea-going engineer that Gef appeared to be a mongoose; but the question which arises in my mind is, does a mongoose have hands such as Gef possesses? On no single occasion have we ever seen him for a time exceeding two or three seconds."

The best description of Gef by anyone not a member of the Irving household is that of a schoolboy named Cub bon, who lived two miles from Doarlish Cashen. Irving declares that this boy told him: "I saw Gef in a field behind Gordon Chapel. He was little and had a flat face, yellow, and a big bushy tail at him" ("at him" is the Manx idiomatic expression for "he had"). The latest extant description of Gef's physical appearance tallies closely with the earlier accounts given by Irving in his letters. This description was sent by Irving in September 1935, in response to a request for details which would enable an artist's sketch of Gef to be drawn.

Length of body: 6 inches.

Tail, 6 inches. Shape of body: Similar almost to a ferret.

Shape of tail: As a squirrel.

Legs are very short, the front ones terminate in a hand of three long fingers and a thumb, and apparently devoid of hair. Hind legs short. Shape of feet unknown to us except from plastic impress in your possession.

Colour of body and tail: Light yellow or biscuit; but the extreme tip of tail has a well-marked tuft of dark brown hair. Coat of fur is long and very fine, giving a fluffy appearance.

Whiskers (as a rabbit).

Eyebrows: Long and coarse hair, very dark.

GEF THE TALKING MONGOOSE

Eyes: Blue (as to colour; Gef says blue, we ourselves cannot say).

Face: Profile as a squirrel (ears short), but if anything more pointed. What is important, the nose is flattened at the end after the manner somewhat of a pig.

My wife and daughter have both had good views of his full face. I have only had a view of his profile.

When Gef is in motion, sometimes the tail is held out in a direct line with the body, at other times carried over the back exactly as a squirrel.

Circumference of body is extremely small, and I have reason to believe he could pass through a round hole of six or seven inches in circumference.

Weight (pure guess, of course): Cannot exceed 2 lb.

Speed when running: Like a flash. Strength enormous; entirely out of proportion to his size. His strength both my wife and self can vouch for by actual experiences.

The measurements of the body and tail were supplied by Gef himself this morning (2nd September 1935) and are just about as we would all assume.

Ever since the early days of his career at Doarlish Cashen, Gef has manifested an almost unconquerable dislike to being seen. For some months at first it was difficult to make him leave the shelter of the upper story of the farm-house, and still more to come out into the open air. Irving records that "At the end of 1931 and early in 1932, I used to lie in bed listening to Gef and looking about the room for him, when Gef would complain I was looking at him."

On June 7th 1932 he writes that "On April 30 Gef was persuaded to run on the cross-beams which support the roof . . . and as we had a fair view [we] are able to give a little more detail as to his appearance."

Less than a fortnight afterwards Gef had become more adventurous, but was still shy of being seen. "He has spoken outside the house to strangers, as well as inside," says Irving, "but as yet we cannot induce him to show himself."

There is some inconsistency here in the facts as Irving recollects them, for in November 1934 he narrates an incident in 1931, which shows that at that time Gef was "extending his range of activities well beyond the confines of Doarlish Cashen."

In December 1931 he says, in the absence from home of Mrs. Irving, he went down to fetch Voirrey home from the local schoolhouse at Glen Maye. After a conversation with Miss Creer, the schoolmistress, he was returning with his daughter up the steep path to Doarlish Cashen, when Gef's voice was heard peremptorily demanding: "What did you tell Miss Creer about me?" Irving adds that "about this same time, winter 1931- 2, road repairs were being effected in the neighbourhood. Gef was daily watching the men at work, and was telling [us] all they spoke about, horse-racing, etc."

One of the work- men saw what was assumed to be Gef take a piece of bread he had thrown away during his dinner. The visual evidence of Gef's existence is complicated by certain doubts which Irving has from time to time expressed as to whether Gef (a) is capable of assuming varied animal forms, and (b) can render himself invisible. Sometimes Gef has appeared to Irving in the form of what he thought was a cat; or, on another occasion, a polecat (skunk).

GEF THE TALKING MONGOOSE

"As regards invisibility," Irving has told us, "this is a matter I have often debated with my wife long before you mentioned it, but most of our experiences in this connection are very contradictory. One moment we say 'Yes', and then in another moment 'No.' Even Gef's answers to our queries are contradictory. If I ask him point-blank if he can make himself invisible, he says 'No.' But again if I tell him to keep away from a certain place, for fear the dogs will seize him, he says: 'They'll never see me.'. . . . Although he is at the bus depot daily and for hours, they have never seen him; the night-watchman on one occasion saw his shadow, and this man (Leece) was at another time struck with an iron nut, and the man got the wind up. Gale, the controller, told me of the foregoing. I saw the man Leece afterwards and he confirmed it. . . The fact that Gef can enter and leave my house, as he has done hundreds of times, without being seen by us, look as often as we like, compels us to think that invisibility is a possibility."

In the course of his four years at Doarlish Cashen, Gef has certainly advanced some distance towards overcoming his shyness of being seen. Even now there is no human witness outside of the Irving family who will come forward to testify to having seen him face to face. He has, however, after much coquettish hesitation, permitted himself to be interviewed by one non-human witness – the camera. Not until after our visit to Doarlish Cashen in July 1935, when we presented a new Kodak to Voirrey, were clear photographs of Gef forthcoming. They purport to show Gef perched upon the top of a sod hedge near the farm. There is no question of these photographs being faked, in the sense of any manipulation of the camera, negatives, or prints. But the reader will draw his own conclusions as to how much they add to our visual knowledge of Gef. Contenting ourselves here with saying that it is not easy to make out any animal form in these pictures, we will leave them for final consideration at a later point in this analysis.

So much for the visual evidence of Gef's existence – scanty and in some degree unsatisfactory. The aural evidence, on the contrary, is much greater in amount, more varied in character, and more convincing. Gef began to speak intelligibly sometime in the autumn of 1931, so Irving tells us, and has continued – with short intervals due to absence or sullenness – to talk ever since, to the Irvings, to various visitors, and above all to Captain Macdonald.

At the outset we are faced with the problem of grasping the precise method by which Gef learned from Irving how to talk. He began by making "animal noises" behind the match-boarding at Doarlish Cashen; next he reproduced Irving's voice when the latter imitated the calls of various animals; then Voirrey induced Gef to repeat nursery rhymes; and finally Gef learned from Irving to converse fully in English. It is a pity that no outsider could have been present to listen to these strange lessons in elocution.

To judge from the time taken to master English – a few days only, according to Irving – Gef must have been a highly intelligent pupil. He afterwards told his teacher that he had been able to understand English, though not to speak it, before he came to Doarlish Cashen. As regards the nature of Gef's voice, Irving has told us that it is shrill and whistling, which Captain Macdonald confirms in his report, where he refers to "a very shrill voice" and "the shrill, piping voice" that he heard upstairs. Sometimes, says Irving, Gef's voice is so shrill as to be not easily intelligible by strangers. It is characteristic of the voice that its place of origin is not easily located. It may appear to come first from one corner of the house or room, and then suddenly from another – the change being so rapid as to give no time for Gef to have changed his bodily position accordingly. Irving narrates how, when he was one day watching Voirrey milk the goats some four or five yards from the house porch, "Gef was calling to us both, the voice apparently proceeding from under the high cement step. His voice appears to be where his body is not." This elusiveness persists out of doors as well as indoors. "Out of doors, when walking side by side by Voirrey, Gef's voice appears to be in the air, and not a foot away from the back of my head. Indoors, the voice moves about as quick as wireless, so rapidly in fact that obstructions to his bodily movements do not seem to exist."

Gef also appears to possess acute hearing which enables him to repeat what is being said at a distance from him. One Sunday, says Irving, "my wife and I were in the goat-house, conversing about nothing in particular, and very quietly too. Gef was under the slate roof of the porch, calling out all my wife was saying, word for word. I have stepped the distance, and it is sixty feet away. He did not repeat anything I was saying."

Apparently, there are certain stimuli to which Gef regularly responds, in regard to his speaking. He is more attracted to the female than the male portion of the Irving family. "Mrs. Irving is an attraction for Gef," Irving has told us, "but Voirrey is the attraction, and it is from her that he draws his ability to speak, although he but rarely speaks to her direct."

From the earliest days of the haunting Gef followed Voirrey about, apparently interested in her movements and doings; yet he converses much more often with her parents than with her. The phrase, "It is from her (Voirrey) that he draws his ability to speak", is rather curious, in view of Irving's insistence that it was he who taught Gef to talk in the first place. Apparently what is meant is that the emotional stimulus comes (or came) from Voirrey, the intellectual stimulus from Irving himself.

Gef's attraction to Mrs. Irving seems based on the fact that it is she, principally, who supplies him with food. In the course of his four years' career at Doarlish Cashen, Gef's affections have become somewhat modified. Originally he was essentially attracted to Voirrey, and was indifferent or hostile to her parents; now he has become, says Irving, much attached to him and his wife, while the attraction to Voirrey, though persisting, is cooler. On Voirrey's side, certainly, the attraction is no longer reciprocated. However interested she may have once been in Gef, she now professes indifference to his movements and behaviour, and has told us she would not care if he went away and never returned to Doarlish Cashen.

The Irvings claim that they "can influence, but cannot control Gef entirely". This means, first, that they cannot make him speak to them individually or collectively just when and how they please; and second, that they cannot make him speak to order to strangers. Apparently most of Gef's conversations – Irving says 90 per cent – have been carried on when two or more members of the Irving family were present. Only once in a blue moon does he speak to either Irving, Mrs. Irving, or Voirrey alone; and but for these exceptions Irving would have concluded long ago that, for some unknown reason, Gef could or would only speak when there was a combination of two or three of them present. Sometimes, as in November 1934, he talks in the presence of the whole family; but more often, it appears, he speaks when either Voirrey and her father, or Voirrey and her mother, are together.

Nocturnally, Gef also speaks and plays pranks upon or about the cross-beam dividing the bedroom occupied by Mr. and Mrs. Irving from the bedroom occupied by Voirrey. Gef's "sanctum", upon which he dances and pushes about furniture, is situated in Voirrey's room. And it must be remembered that, to use Irving's words, "practically all his (Gef's) talking is done after we have all retired to rest and the light extinguished. Then he starts, and it lasts anything from half an hour to an hour."

In December 1931, when relations with Gef were still in an unfriendly and suspicious stage, he displayed furious anger towards Mr. and Mrs. Irving for insisting upon moving their daughter's bed into their own room, out of fear lest Gef should do her some mischief. All this, together with the admitted "bond of interest" existing between Voirrey and Gef, has led some observers to suppose that Gef could only speak when Voirrey was present.

Irving himself is aware of these opinions, for he has told us: "I have many times questioned Gef, and asked him could he not speak if Voirrey were not present. He was very indignant and said: 'Of course I can, and I have done so'; and he most certainly has spoken when Voirrey has not been within a mile of Gef."

Irving has recorded a number of instances of such utterances. One day, in the middle of June 1934, he says: "My wife and I took a stroll round one or two of my fields, leaving Voirrey indoors, and whilst we were away Gef called us from a few yards distance close by the sod hedges." Again, on July 9th, about 1 p.m, Gef whistled and halloed from around one of the outbuildings to Mrs. Irving and Voirrey while they were in the kitchen of the farmhouse; Gef could hear what Mrs. Irving was saying, and kept on repeating her words.

GEF THE TALKING MONGOOSE

This capacity of Gef to speak when Voirrey is absent is particularly emphasized by Irving in the report which he drafted for Captain Macdonald after the latter's second visit to Doarlish Cashen. "Now what I wish to impress upon you is this," he tells Captain Macdonald. "In these two experiences you have had what no one else has had (excepting ourselves), that is, you heard him speak in the house whilst my daughter was out of the house a hundred feet away), and he spoke to us both, outside the house and when my daughter was in the house. Many people have heard Gef speak in the house, whilst Voirrey was not in, but no one else has heard him speak outside the house and Voirrey inside, so that your dual experiences in this respect are absolutely 'unique', and you have been very fortunate."

In the two experiences referred to Captain Macdonald heard Gef speak first when he (Captain Macdonald) and Mr. and Mrs. Irving were indoors, while Voirrey was outside attending to sitting hens in the stackyard; and secondly, when he (Captain Macdonald) and Irving were on their way down to Glen Maye, about eighty paces from the house, in which they had left Mrs. Irving and Voirrey. As regards displaying his vocal powers to strangers generally Gef is highly suspicious, and will not as a rule manifest himself to those whom he dubs "doubters", or to groups of people.

(Irving is rather fond of telling visitors to Doarlish Cashen who have heard Gef that they have been specially privileged, and that their experiences have been "unique".)

Gef prefers to speak when one stranger is present, and that one a believer in his existence, or at least not a sceptic. His utterances to such persons usually take one of three forms…(a) the penny trick, first apparently played on July 20th 1934, for the benefit of two young visitors from Wavertree; (b) shutting one of the house doors from the outside when part or the whole of the company present is inside the house or one of its rooms; (c) calling "coo-ee" when the visitor is at some point on the path from Glen Maye, the call sounding as if it came from behind the sod hedges which enclose the path.

Another favourite form taken by Gef's utterances is the repeating of words and phrases supposed to have been said by the visitor in private, either to his friends, or to one of the Irvings. Thus Gef claims the power to read thoughts; there is evidence, however, that he over-estimates this power and often falls into inaccuracies, reporting sentences that have never been spoken. According to Irving, Gef used at one time to practise this kind of "magic" upon Irving himself.

"Whilst in one way his talking is wonderful," he tells us, "as is also his general knowledge, yet his magic, as he calls it, is more wonderful still. I can grasp the idea of speech and knowledge, but his magic is quite beyond me. I refer to his being able to record my movements about the place, out of sight and out of sound, and Gef indoors all the time. If Gef will reveal how he can tell, that will be a step nearer to knowing what he really is."

An example of this "magic" occurred on June 7th 1934, when, while Irving was clipping sheep about two hundred and fifty yards from the house and out of sight of it, Gef was conversing at home with Mrs. Irving and Voirrey, telling the former which sheep Irving was actually clipping. But on no occasion, adds Irving, has Gef ever recorded the movements out of doors of either Mrs. Irving or Voirrey.

And this brings us to a consideration of the character of Gef's utterances in general. The number of his sayings put on record by Irving in his letters, diaries, and conversations is prodigious; they would easily fill a small book. But they can be mainly classified into two categories: (1) First, opinions, information, and words obviously acquired from Irving himself. This is not surprising, since Irving has taught Gef to speak in the first place. If, then, Gef uses Manx, Russian, Hindustani, or other foreign words it is because Irving too has a smattering of these languages. Gef's conversation, in short, reflects largely what goes on in Irving's own mind. (2) Second, information or gossip concerning the doings of neighbours or villagers within a radius of twenty miles of Glen Maye, collected by Gef in the course of his rambles, and brought home to retell to the Irvings. In this part of his conversation Gef appears to reflect much more the interests of Voirrey. He concerns himself particularly with the bus depot at Peel, and reports what the motor mechanics and depot manager say. He talks of the air-service officials, of gangs of men doing road repairs, of village gatherings and festivities. If there was a member of the Irving household going about the countryside and mingling with the neighbours, this is the kind of gossip which that member might be expected to bring back home.

We may round off this account of Gef's aural manifestations by an assessment of the experiences of Captain Macdonald. On his first visit to Doarlish Cashen in February 1932, the Captain heard sounds, but was only partly convinced that they emanated from Gef or proved Gef's existence. "I don't quite know what I really think," he concluded, "as the attitude of the Irvings has rather defeated me." This evidently refers to the fact that Voirrey and Mrs. Irving had to go upstairs together to induce Gef to begin talking from the bedroom. For some time after his visit Captain Macdonald continued to correspond with Irving, receiving from him extracts from his diary, and various detailed accounts of Gef's activities.

After about ten months, however, this correspondence died away, and from February 16th 1933 to the end of March 1934 little was heard of Gef – in fact, those who, like the director of the *Isle of Man Examiner*, had taken an interest in his doings during 1932 were led to suppose that he had ceased his hauntings. But in the spring of 1934 Irving began again to correspond regularly with Captain Macdonald, and before long had laid so many fresh facts before the Captain that the latter's curiosity was roused afresh, and he determined to journey a second time to Glen Maye. This time he stayed longer, and was led by what he heard to take a much more favourable view of Gef's reality.

Captain Macdonald was regaled by Gef with a performance of his penny trick, with a demonstration of thought-reading, with utterances inside the living-room, and calls of "coo-ee" outside the house. In fact, Gef ranged the full gamut of his capacities, leaving only room for improvement in the degree, rather than the kind, of his vocalizing. When heard indoors, "the voice was but a few feet away, and behind the wainscot". When heard out of doors (at midnight), Gef's voice was about eighty paces from the house. Irving and the Captain disagreed at first as to where the sound came from, but subsequently Irving agreed with the Captain that it came from a gap in the sod hedge about ten feet away from where they were walking.

Upon the occasion of Captain Macdonald's third visit to Doarlish Cashen, the manifestations of Gef were much more striking than before. Raps, bangs, knockings and shrill screams filled the house; a bottle and tray were flung at the Captain's head, and furniture thrown about in Voirrey's room. As on the occasion of his second visit, Captain Macdonald's tactics were to try and "catch" the voice by stealing up to the part of the house from which it appeared to be corning and flashing his hand torch upon it. Both times he failed completely, leaving one to conclude either that there was only a disembodied voice about the place or that Gef could move too quickly for the human eye.

Supplementing his written report, Captain Macdonald has told us that, on the last occasion he tried to take Gef by surprise, by running to the stairs and flashing his torch up them, he gained a glimpse of the panel of Voirrey's bedroom door shaking as if something had struck it. This he supposed to be due to Gef's having bounced against the door in his fright, and then rebounded off into the Irvings' bedroom opposite. But the shaking of the door in this way is also susceptible of another explanation – that Voirrey was not so well secured in her bedroom as the Captain supposed. It has already been noted in an earlier chapter that not once, in all his visits, has Captain Macdonald heard Gef when all the members of the Irving family were present at the same moment in the room with him and under his observation. Mr. Northwood, however, is positive that, on the occasion of his visit to Doarlish Cashen in March 1932 Voirrey and Irving were both seated at the tea-table with him (Mrs. Irving being away from home at the time) when Gef's voice was heard coming from behind the panelling. And Mr. Northwood's son, Arthur, had a similar experience later on the same day.

Captain Macdonald, We may observe, was also much impressed by the showers of pebbles and sand which were thrown at the windows of the porch, etc., from outside, at about three o'clock in the morning at the end of the violent happenings described above. He considers that this was proof of supernatural agency, since all the members of the Irving family were indoors at the time, Voirrey in bed, and her parents below with him in the sitting-room. However, readers of this book will by now have fully examined the reports of these episodes, and must determine for themselves whether or not they would be convinced by similar experiences.

Besides the visual and the aural evidence for Gef, there remain certain indirect pieces of evidence of a material kind. Gef is said to take food from the Irvings, though his diet is certainly more luxurious than nourishing. He urinates (Captain Macdonald and others have been shown signs of this on the wall of the house), but does not excrete. He has been touched and felt by the members of the Irving family-though not by anyone else. His teeth have once drawn blood from Mrs. Irving's finger – in spite of which, however, she has persisted in feeling his teeth again on several occasions since then.

Gef has displayed animosity against visitors with whom he was displeased, by spitting upon them; he has also, more playfully; thrown stones, sand, pins, and other objects at the backs of members of the Irving family and at visitors. During our own visit to Doarlish Cashen we were shown, and took away with us, several such apports, including certain small wooden objects which are apparently Indian chessmen or draughtsmen, made of boxwood, and possibly turned on a native Indian lathe. More impressive are the tufts of hair and eyebrows sent by Irving to Captain Macdonald and Mr. Price in May 1935, and said to have been placed by Gef in a jar on the shelf above the fire-place in the living-room ofDoarlish Cashen, in response to Irving's request for further proofs of his identity. But laboratory tests -have shown that these hairs are not those of a mongoose, but, according to expert opinion, are identical with other hairs which we ourselves took from the different parts of the body of the dog Mona while we were at Doarlish Cashen.

Summing up the three kinds of evidence (visual, aural, and tangible) it is clear that they are more impressive when taken together, by reason of their cumulative bulk and mutual consistency than they are when analysed separately. The visual evidence by itself, resting only upon what members of the Irving family have seen, would not carry conviction to the ordinary man who had seen nothing for himself.

The tangible evidence, when it does not rest only upon what members of the Irving family say they have felt, is also only circumstantial, and in more than one example open to suspicion. Consequently, the reality of Gef's existence stands or falls by the aural evidence. Now aural evidence by its very nature is less satisfactory than visual or tangible evidence, because it is more open to the interpretation of being imagined or fabricated. In this case the testimony of the Irving family is backed up by the independent testimony of Captain Macdonald. Again we come back to the point that, in default of other witnesses coming forward with a written statement of their experiences, only from Captain Macdonald's reports and from Mr. Northwood's notes can we deduce an opinion. Captain Macdonald believes he heard Gef. Was he, a solitary independent witness, in a position to feel absolutely certain that what he heard in the company of one or more members of the Irving family was really Gef? Again, was he convinced that no other but a supernatural explanation was possible of what he heard, i.e. of the manifestations attributed to Gef? If these two queries be answered in the affirmative, then we must certainly – in view of the antecedents, attainments, and character of Captain Macdonald, and in view of the corroborative testimony of Mr. Northwood, admit that Gef's reality is in a fair way towards being proved.

But supposing we agree that Gef really haunts Doarlish Cashen, and that all, or even part, of what is told us of his sayings and doings is true – then, how are we explain what Gef is? Let us begin with some recapitulation of the Irvings' own theories about Gef, since they have had more opportunity than anyone else to form an opinion on this point. If we look back to the summer of 1932 we find that at that time Irving – as seems natural – was still toying with the idea that Gef must be some sort of animal, unusual and extraordinary no doubt, but still an animal. "Undoubtedly he is a species of mongoose," he declares on June 7th, "but whether a hybrid or not, I cannot say. Whatever it is, animal or spirit, it is an unheard-of thing before." Exactly what first led Irving to identify Gef as a mongoose is uncertain; but we must remember that living specimens of mongoose had actually been let loose years before in the district of Glen Maye by a neighbouring farmer with a name similar to Irving's.

At the end of 1932 we find Irving still clinging to the theory that Gef is an animal, but without much conviction. Seeking for some evidence, however slender, that a mongoose might be able to talk, he consults a friend on the Liverpool Cotton Exchange, who tells him that the fakirs in India possess the power of making mongooses speak; a little later he hears from a lady whose Anglo-Indian acquaintance assures her mongooses can talk and have a human brain—but are very shy!

Apparently Irving withstood for some time the suggestion that Gef might be a spirit—even though this suggestion came from Gef himself. For during the winter of 1931-1932 one of Gef's favourite expressions, repeated, in the words of Irving, ad nauseam, was: "I am a ghost in the form of a weasel, and I'll haunt you." However, early in 1932 a "spiritualistic investigator" from England visited Doarlish Cashen, and told Irving that "What you have seen and heard of him [Gef] is not an animal, it is a spirit". The investigator subsequently explained in a letter that Gef must be an earthbound spirit which had taken on the form of a mongoose, and had been attracted to the Irving family by the encouragement he had received from them. This explanation seems to have met with Irving's approval, as he has constantly reiterated it ever since in his correspondence and conversation. No doubt it received confirmation from Captain Macdonald, who seems to have adopted it also after his first visit. "Many people", writes Irving to him in April 1934, "have suggested to me that he must be a spirit. I think you were of that opinion, so I have often put it to him and asked him if he were. He always answers: 'I am not a spirit; if I were I could not kill rabbits.'"

The undeniable force of this argument seems to have had its effect on Irving, who none the less admits in the same letter that he has twice heard Gef say: 'I am an earth-bound spirit', in direct contradiction to his more usual account of himself. As a rule Gef will admit to being nothing more than a clever animal. 'I'm not a spirit,' he replied to Irving's questions, 'I am a little extra, extra clever mongoose.' But Irving argues with him that he must be a spirit, or he could not have the knowledge which he possesses; and to this retort Gef returns evasive replies.

In June 1934 a party of five people, including two active spiritualists from Chester, visited Doarlish Cashen, the latter assuring Irving positively that Gef must be a spirit; but they "are somewhat nonplussed when I told them that it ate our food. All the same, these people adhered to it that it is a spirit and in this form and that Gef could dematerialize himself. Whether he can or not, I do not know. The statement is theirs, not mine."

By this time Irving is inclining himself strongly to the "spirit" hypothesis. "Really, the only visitors we have had who understand what Gef is (beyond an animal)," he writes to Captain Macdonald, "are people like yourself, and not more than five or six at the outside." Towards the end of 1934 he is inclining towards the notion of reincarnation. "He must be, as you state, a spirit of a hitherto unheard-of or rare kind. He must have been on earth before as a human, which accounts for his knowledge, intelligence, fluency, love of music, and other abilities which are only found in humans."

This idea haunts Irving's mind, and he develops his new thesis a week later. "Is it not possible that Gef is the spirit of someone who has departed this life, and is not aware of it? My wife particularly thinks he does know all about his previous existence, but will not admit it. If he is a spirit in this form, are not our chances of getting him to show himself to others just about nil?"

The "earth-bound spirit" hypothesis, varied occasionally by queries as to the possibility of Gef's being a "hybrid" type of mongoose, or super-animal, is Irving's chief contribution towards accounting for the mysterious being that haunts his house. His difficulty in finding a consistent and satisfying label for Gef has no doubt been intensified by Gef's own inconsistency about himself. Generally, Gef denies that he is a spirit of any sort; he even dislikes all references to ghosts and spirits, and upon one occasion compelled Irving to tear up a book of ghost stories that had been brought into the house. But sometimes Gef has lapses; he claims for himself magical powers, threatens to "haunt" the Irvings, and admits to being a "freak" and even on rare occasions a spirit. Clearly no solution is to be sought here. Any convincing interpretation of what Gef is must be sought for outside, and not inside, Doarlish Cashen.

CHAPTER V

SPECULATIONS ABOUT GEF

MANY of the events related by Irving can be classified by those experienced in psychical research as belonging to the class of 'poltergeist' phenomena. Amongst these are Gef's habit of throwing sand and small stones, also metal, wooden, and bone objects, at persons in or near Doarlish Cashen; the thumping, scratching, rapping, and banging noises which he makes behind the panelling and ·in the rafters of the house; and the movement of furniture . It is a common feature of the numerous cases of this sort that the household having these experiences should include a young person passing through puberty, and the theory has been advanced that there may be some connection between the vital forces thus upsurging in the adolescent and the physical disturbances. Moreover, since, during the period of the haunting, the household at Doarlish Cashen has included a young girl, brought up in a rather peculiar environment, it might be supposed that here we have yet another poltergeist case, which should be examined, recorded, and classified as such. Unfortunately, the matter is not even as simple as that. The only historic poltergeist that bears much resemblance to Gef is that which in 1716 and 1717 afflicted the household of Jo n Wesley at Epworth Vicarage. This lasted for several months, and took, the form chiefly of rapping's and knockings. There are certain odd points of apparent similarity to Gef. In the first place, the Epworth poltergeist was known to the Wesley family as "Jeffery", and is constantly referred to by that name in their correspondence.

In the next place, the manifestations were observed to be closely connected with one of the seven daughters of the household, Hetty Wesley. To the other members of the family "Jeffery" manifested himself chiefly as a noise – such as a sound of walking in the room overhead, a sound like the winding of a jack or like a carpenter planing deal boards. Only Hetty maintained she had actually seen him in animal form, looking like a badger, under her bed. Samuel Wesley, too, heard something more than mere knocks or raps; he described it as "two or three feeble squeaks a little louder than the chirping of a bird", which might pass, according to some witnesses, as not a bad description of some of the utterances at Doarlish Cashen. Whether "Jeffery" was an ancestor of "Gef" will never be known; but it is certain that the differences between the two are much greater than the resemblances.

(See Adam Clarke, *Memoirs of the Wesley Family*, London, 1823.)

Gef indeed will hardly bear classification as a poltergeist at all, for in the whole history of such phenomena there is no known case of a poltergeist assuming the form of a talking animal, and conversing with human beings intelligently and at length. To find any parallel with Gef in history we have to go back to the seventeenth century, to the "familiars" which witches confessed to nurturing and using for their baneful purposes; and even these "familiars" possessed nothing like the conversational powers of Gef. It is indeed the vocal powers which give the hauntings at Doarlish Cashen their special peculiarity, together with their attribution to an "animal" – a talking mongoose. But the existence of the bodily form of this animal is itself rather shadowy, since no one apart from the Irvings has seen it, and the secondary evidences for it (hair, paw and teeth marks, and photographs) are unconvincing. If, then, we leave out of our reckoning for the moment the animal authorship of the sounds, we are left with at any rate a "voice" to account for – for that there is a voice, and that it utters intelligible sounds, and can converse in various languages with other persons, must be held to be proven unless Captain Macdonald, Mr. Northwood, and other independent witnesses are all victims of hallucination.

The voice seems to emanate, firstly, from behind the panelling at Doarlish Cashen, and next from behind sod hedges out in the open away from Doarlish Cashen. In the course of our investigation we frequently came across the suggestion that Gef's voice is a product of ventriloquism, and that Voirrey Irving possesses ventriloquial powers. This suggestion was given currency by the newspapers during the winter 1931-1932, when the tide of popular interest in the "spook" at Glen Maye was running high, and reporters who came over and interviewed the Irving family were doing their best to explain away the mysterious sounds. At that time it was noted – what has always been admitted by the Irving family – that Gef had an affinity or attraction for Voirrey, and seemed to go where she went and to speak usually when she wished. From this it was but a step to argue that Voirrey must be a "natural ventriloquist". But we find it difficult to accept this explanation, however plausible it may appear. For an examination of any text-book of ventriloquism will show that there is no such thing as a born, or natural, ventriloquist, any more than there is a born, or natural, stenographer or piano-player. The art must be acquired by long practice, is less easily acquired by women than by men, and by children or adolescents than by adults. Furthermore, the idea that a ventriloquist can throw his voice to any place, within hearing, that he may select is quite exploded. He simply modulates his voice so as to make it sound to his hearers to proceed from the spot to which he directs their attention. To be a good ventriloquist you must be an actor, and those who have had stage training are undoubtedly the best ventriloquists.

(Hercat's Ventriloquist (1916), p . 20. Published by Dean and Son Ltd., IS.)

There are, it is true, some episodes in the career of Gef – for instance, his imitation of farmyard animal noises made by Irving in 1931 – which might suggest a ventriloquial origin. But the majority of the sounds made by Gef cannot be accounted for thus, particularly those which occur in the dark. As Frederic MacCabe, one of the most famous of ventriloquists put it: "All the illusions of ventriloquism depend very much on the imagination of the hearers. The power of imitating sound is only part of the art. The effect of ventriloquism is a creation of the imagination produced by the deception of the ear and the eyes. The attention of the hearer must be caught by little indescribable actions and tricks of manner and directed to the spot from whence the sound is supposed to proceed. The effect to be produced must be suggested to the mind at the moment that the sound is imitated, and the imagination of the audience thus made to help on the illusion."

(Ventriloquism and Kindred Arts, p. 39. By Fred Russell. Published by Keith Prowse.)

Thus Gef's voice could not be made to come from out of the darkness, for instance, on the way down from Doarlish Cashen to Glen Maye late at night. Nor could his voice be made, by ventriloquism, to sound from different parts of the house at Doarlish Cashen, in the absence of the member of the family who is supposed to be able to ventriloquize.

Jim Irving using a pair of knives to show the depth of a crack in the matchboard paneling from where Gef threw a packing needle at Capt. Mcdonald.

GEF THE TALKING MONGOOSE

While abandoning this purely ventriloquial explanation of Gef, we may nevertheless note that the voice which emanates from behind the panelling resembles in some of its features the Saragossa Ghost which made such a stir in the world's newspapers during November and December 1934. The inhabitants of a second-floor flat in the Calle Gascon de Gotor, a street on the outskirts of Saragossa in Spain, were terrified by a mysterious voice emanating from the chimney or flue of their kitchen range. The voice talked in daylight, seemed to be friendly, and possessed great fluency and a sense of humour. Soon the affair became a nine days' wonder, and the flat was invaded by sightseers; but at last the police were called in and a magistrate undertook an investigation. The chimney or flue from which the voice emanated served eight other flats in the same house; but the voice addressed itself chiefly to one set of tenants, a family named Palazon, who employed a sixteen-year-old servant girl named Maria Pascuela. Suspicion soon connected this girl with the voice. Various tests were made, and a report drawn up – which apparently suggested that the girl was responsible for the sounds, either by means of ventriloquism, or because she was a medium. In each case it was said that she was "unconscious" of what she was doing.

The explanation of the Saragossa Ghost is incomplete, but it suggests certain trains of thought as regards the haunting of Doarlish Cashen. The voice in the flat in the Calle Gascon de Sotor was connected in some way with a human person, but it reached its hearers through the medium of a flue or chimney. Does there exist at Doarlish Cashen any human person with whom Gef's voice might be similarly connected, and any sounding mechanism through which that voice might be transmitted? There is no wireless set at Doarlish Cashen. There is a gramophone. But neither of these would be capable of the number and variety of utterances made by

Gef. However, there is also something comparable with the Saragossa flue – and that is the panelling at Doarlish Cashen. Without making a series of tests on the spot it would not be right to dogmatize on this point; but from a cursory examination of the panelling and the several places where it had been opened, we may reasonably suppose that the space between the walls and the panelling could well serve as a kind of megaphone or loud-speaker. If this be so, a voice speaking into a crack or hole in the panelling at one place might be heard at another spot, or in another room in the same house. There are, of course, numerous fissures and holes of this kind in the bedrooms, living-room, and pantry of Doarlish Cashen. We also noticed many cracks and small holes on the exterior of the house, particularly in the foundations.

To eliminate the possibility of some such "natural" transmission of Gef's voice, it would seem to be necessary that Gef should be heard by one or (preferably) more visitors at a time when all the members of the household were present within actual sight of these visitors, and when no outsider was in the neighbourhood of the house. (This latter condition could be easily fulfilled, since, as there are no trees or shrubs near Doarlish Cashen, it would be difficult for a stranger to approach or hide nearby without being observed.) So far as we can trace, there is no recorded occasion on which all these conditions have been indisputably fulfilled.

The transmission of Gef's voice through the panelling is consistent with certain points deducible from Irving's own narrative. One of these is Gef's choice of Doarlish Cashen for his residence because "the house suits me". Another is the apparently rapid movements of Gef behind the panelling, following the sound of his voice, which seems to flit about from place to place. A third is the quality of the sound itself – its shrillness and high whistling note, all what one would expect as coming from a kind of speaking-tube.

But to find a "natural" explanation of the voice of Gef inside Doarlish Cashen is one thing, and to account for that voice as heard out in the open, away from Doarlish Cashen, is another. Obviously, no panelling could help in the latter case. Here we must first ask where the voice was actually heard. On the occasion of Captain Macdonald's second visit (May 1935), according to Irving, "we had reached a point eighty paces away (I stepped it) when Gef called out 'coo-ee' to us". Subsequently Gef informed Irving that he had been ten feet distant from them when he spoke. This is typical of the various occasions on which this phenomenon was experienced. One may say that, as a rule, when Gef speaks or calls out of doors, it is within a short radius; say under a hundred yards, of Doarlish Cashen. Upon one or two occasions calls at a farther distance have been recorded, but no coherent sentences have been uttered at these times.

Moreover, these "coo-ees" usually occur after dark, either at twilight or about midnight when the visitor is leaving. Theoretically, it would be possible to imagine a person who knew the district well, who had walked over every field and hummock and along every hedge in the neighbourhood, running or creeping the other side of the sod hedges that bound the track leading down the hill-side and making these sounds to impress the visitor. No prolonged conversations take place on these occasions; but the effect of the eerie "coo-ees" is emphasized by Gef's habit of afterwards repeating the conversations that he claims to have overheard while "shadowing" Irving and his visitor. The visitor has heard Gef "coo-ee" in the open; a little later he finds that the household at Doarlish Cashen is fully acquainted with things he has been saying in the imagined privacy of a lonely mountain path. No wonder he is impressed with a sense of Gef's ubiquity. But are the facts susceptible of another and more material explanation?

At this point we may usefully consider what other evidence there is definitely pointing to a materialistic explanation of Gef. First we have the tufts and strands of hair sent by Irving in the summer of 1935, and alleged to have been plucked by Gef from his own eyebrows, sides, and tail, and placed in ajar on the mantelpiece at Doarlish Cashen. This hair Mr. Martin Duncan declares not to have been plucked, but cut off, and to be ascribable not to any mongoose or similar animal, but rather to a sheep-dog or collie dog. Armed with this information, we ourselves brought back from Doarlish Cashen certain tufts of hair which we cut off from the coat of Mona, the Irvings' collie dog. Now, having microscopically examined these latter tufts, Mr. Martin Duncan declares himself satisfied that they come from the same source as the alleged tufts of Gef's hair – that is from Mona. We are entitled to conclude that the hair sent by Irving was not hair from Gef, but hair from Mona. How this mistake occurred – whether, perhaps, Gef in one of his freakish moods was playing a crude practical joke upon his landlord we cannot say. But the expert's analysis and conclusion stand, and under- mine one of the main pieces of tangible evidence for Gef's existence.

In the next place, we have the paw prints and teeth marks in dough and plasticine, sent by Irving during August 1935, after our abortive visit to Doarlish Cashen at the end of July. Upon receipt of these prints we were at once struck – as will be any reader who consults the photograph – by the disparity in the size and shape of the markings. Two of the paw marks, though discrepant with each other, are much larger than the third. According to Irving the larger marks represent the front, the smaller the hind paws of Gef. These paw and teeth prints we dispatched to Mr. R. I. Pocock, who in due course reported that one of the paw prints might conceivably be "a raccoon's and another a dog's, but that there is no mammal in which there is such disparity in the size of the fore and hind foot", and finally that "I do not believe these photographs represent foot tracks at all. Most certainly none of them was made by a mongoose." Another expert in finger-prints to whom we submitted the impressions gave a similar opinion, grounded on the fact that the marks showed no signs of skin texture, and therefore could not have been made by any animal.

All this is conclusive testimony, if not to Gef's unreality, at least to his proneness to deceit. But we have ,a third piece of evidence of his existence, of a still more extraordinary character, in the photographs to which reference has been made, which were taken by Voirrey after our visit to Doarlish Cashen, with the camera and spools of film presented by us to her on that occasion. These snapshots are supposed to represent Gef sitting at the top of one of the sod hedges near the farm. We are told that Gef displayed great nervousness on these occasions, constantly spoiling the pictures by leaping down or vanishing at the moment of exposure.

However, we were in due course sent several spools of film, which we had developed and printed. The reader's reaction upon first seeing this print will be what ours was – that no animal can be seen. When examined, the dark objects jutting up above the skyline can be identified as pieces of wood or stone, placed there accidentally or on purpose. When, however, we pointed out to Irving the unconvincing character of these photographs, he did not cease to maintain that they contained true representations of Gef; and, in order to convince us, he had one of them enlarged, and sent us each a copy of the enlargement with an accompanying "key" in the form of a rough pen and ink sketch, and a direction to hold the photograph up to the light. In these enlargements it is possible, without too much stretching of the imagination, to see something which might be a long furry back and tail, half concealed by the grass, and attached to a blunted head and shoulders. According to Irving, Gef's ears and mouth can be seen; the latter holding one or two wisps of grass. Even with this explanation, however, we are afraid the photos of Gef remain unsatisfying. They should be compared with the artist's drawing of Gef which was based upon Irving's detailed verbal description of Gef's physical appearance, and afterwards approved by Gef himself. Do photograph and drawing agree in essentials?

These photographs have suggested to us a hypothesis that has not yet been considered in this book, namely, that the Irving family may be the victims of some kind of hallucination in regard to Gef, who would then have no existence independently of their imagination. A priori, the theory of hallucination seems plausible, in view of the fact that a talking mongoose is a contradiction in terms, a monstrosity as unknown to nature as the centaur or the mermaid, and there- fore to be presumed a figment of the mind. The difficulty is to see how such an hallucination could arise in the minds of a whole family of three persons, all of apparently normal demeanour and intelligence, could be maintained with consistence over so long a period as four years, and finally could be communicated to independent observers in such a way as to carry conviction to them.

(So far as we yet know, sensory hallucinations of several persons together, who are not in an hypnotic state, is a rare phenomenon, and therefore not a probable explanation. -Proceedings of the Society for Psychical Research, Vol. IV, 62.)

GEF THE TALKING MONGOOSE

If we were to construct a theory to account for all this, we should begin by reminding ourselves of the unusual economic and social environment in which the family at Doarlish Cashen has lived for the past twenty years. Isolation, together with lack of many of the occupations which ordinarily fill up a farmer's time, may produce a disposition towards introspection and a tendency to confuse fact and fancy. In the case of Voirrey, particularly, we have a young person even more subjected than her parents to the influence of this unusual environment, since they at any rate have their own past experiences of the outside world to nourish their thoughts. Even in their natural state children are, as is well known to psychologists, often given to imaginative creation; and among such creations are frequently found talking animals of various kinds. Children are attracted to animals, wish they could talk, and easily imagine that they can talk. In fairy-tales animals do talk; and not only children, but grown-ups, cherish fairy-tales and secretly hope that the miracles they relate could be realized in fact. At puberty these fancies often disappear, but sometimes become intensified. Now is it beyond the bounds of possibility that in 1931 Voirrey, at the age of thirteen, may have expressed aloud her belief that a talking animal was inhabiting her home, and may have transferred to this animal the expression of many of her own secret thoughts and hopes?

In support of this we may observe many little similarities between Gef's tastes and opinions and those of Voirrey. Gef likes biscuits, cakes, and sweets-so do young girls. Gef is interested in motor-cars and aeroplanes – so is Voirrey. Gef hunts rabbits – so does Voirrey. Gef roams about the countryside, watching parties of workmen and attending various local social gatherings as a detached observer – all behaviour consonant with what we know of Voirrey. Gef's humour, Gef's wisecracks, Gef's tantrums, Gef's affections –

all have the quality of raw adolescence; and during Gef's tenancy of Doarlish Cashen, Voirrey has been adolescent. None of these things in any way proves an identity between Voirrey's thoughts and Gef; but taken together they lend some degree of plausibility to the theory that he may be her imaginative creation.

Nevertheless, on this hypothesis, it is rather difficult to see how Mr. and Mrs. Irving could have been brought to share a fantasy developed by their daughter. What incentive could rational parents have to indulge any delusion of this sort? Obviously no motive of material gain could enter into the matter-since at no time has Gef brought his owners' any profit, other than a toll of rabbits, and the occasional gifts in kind which his well-wishers and devotees have brought to Doarlish Cashen to propitiate his capricious fancy. Gef is too shy, whimsical, elusive, and. unreliable to be turned to any public account. On the other hand, Gef is distinctly entertaining. Here perhaps we may catch a clue to possible toleration of his presence by the older folk at Doarlish Cashen. Gef's pranks – a little violent and frightening at times – are usually laughable. And in that dark farm-house, particularly when winter-bound, laughter must be rather precious. It may have to go a long way, back and forth, to find subjects. Even as far back as Farmer Irvine (not James T.) and his pack of mongooses, loosed on the countryside long ago to thin the rabbit population. But how easy for a mongoose to jump from one Irving (or Irvine) to another! Particularly when that second Irving has been in his time a traveller, can talk smatterings of many languages, and knows something of India and Egypt – where mongooses come from. Fathers do sometimes indulge their little girls' fancies, and even become proud of them. Families have been known to cherish secret passwords, codes, and legends which have a meaning for their own members, and for no one else. How they all laugh together at the stupid outsider who clumsily seeks to enter the charmed circle, and thinks he has discovered the magic spell! Just as Gef laughs at poor Captain Macdonald. "I might tell Captain Macdonald some of my history, but I will not tell him all. He's damned well not going to get to know my inferior complex."

So we can imagine a tacit alliance springing up between father and daughter, in which Gef's existence is admitted, and he is conversed with, educated, and encouraged to express himself. Gef is a ready learner, and soon comes to interlard his gossip and his wisecracks with scraps of Manx lore, with Hebrew and Hindustani words, with thought-readings and prophecies. "Whatever Gef is, animal only, or a spirit in this form, there has never, I am sure, been anything like it on this earth before." Gef has become unique – more than a mere fairy-tale character. On to adolescent imagination have been grafted adult intelligence and knowledge. And this new Gef can entertain a whole household easily, keep them supplied with amusement throughout a winter – indeed, act for four winters as wireless, cinema, dance-hall, concert, lecturer, court fool, and father-confessor all rolled into one.

The third member of the household is perhaps drawn unresisting into this powerful current. There is such a thing known to psychologists as a folie a deux, where one stronger imagination dominates another less strong, and leads it along a determined path of fantasy. Corroboration and approval are all that are required of the lesser partner; the stronger is the creative influence, the disseminating agent, the justifier of the fantasy. This stronger partner must possess a retentive memory and a persuasive tongue; if to this be added a reputation for probity and a turn for literary expression – then the combination is indeed a strong one, and should go far to win support from visitors who, unconsciously, desire to be convinced of the truth of what they have come so far to investigate.

We can imagine another possible train of events that might carry Gef across the borderline of fiction into the realm of fact. There are times when the desolation and loneliness of Doarlish Cashen must weigh sorely on the spirits of the household-especially the womenfolk, with so few friends to see, and so few opportunities of getting about. What more natural but that the adolescent fantasies of a young girl, when found to be attracting attention from visitors, pressmen, and sightseers, might become imperceptibly enlarged into a permanent fantasy – in the unconscious hope that thereby might arise some occasion of release for loneliness, perhaps even a removal to another and more sociable environment? For Gef has menacing and terrifying, as well as amusing, aspects; and we know that at one time the family was sufficiently frightened by his antics to contemplate being forced to leave their home altogether. If such departure were, after all, not unwelcome to all the household, might not some members of it have tended to invest Gef with greater reality then he really possessed? But perhaps the effect turned out differently from what was intended; perhaps what was conceived and encouraged as a fantasy may have been accepted (unknowingly) as fact – as interesting, desirable, and enjoyable fact – by the very member who should have been dismayed, disconcerted, uprooted by it. Gef as a fantasy may have been turned to ends far from those for which he was conceived.

Now all this is but speculation of our own, the kind of theory that we might conjure up, if we were set upon explaining away Gef as a figment of the imagination. But to do this would surely be to give less than due weight to what we must presume to be altogether beyond figment – that is, the evidence of all those trustworthy outside witnesses who have heard Gef and are certain of his independent existence. Are the three visits of Captain Macdonald, the two visits of Mr. Northwood and his son, and the fairly numerous visits of spiritualists, teachers, hikers, relations, and neighbours all to be put aside and to count for nothing in the scale? It is impossible to deny that there is serious evidence – apart altogether from what the Irvings say – for Gef's reality; such evidence that we can easily believe that had Gef been rather more tractable in his behaviour, less elusive in his manifestations, and more pleasing in his personality he might have become in time the centre of a sort of cult. Already, in spite of his deficiencies, he has gained a tiny circle of admirers eager to hear of his latest doings, ready to pay periodic visits to his shrine, and to being small gifts to propitiate him. It is the stuff of which oracles are made, the foundation upon which temples are built.

But has Gef a future? We doubt it. He rejects spiritistic interpretations of himself, yet will not or cannot reveal his own identity. He has no message to give out, no real miracles to work. His thought-reading appears rather limited, his repertoire of jokes and wisecracks exhaustible. He repeats himself a good deal, and tends to become stale. It is true that he has grown a little bolder as time has gone on – has emerged from t he wainscoting and cross-beams to disport himself in the hedgerows and by-ways of Doarlish Cashen. But Gef has yet to do for outsiders what he has apparently done for the Irvings – show himself to the naked eye, even though he were to remain perched up on the most inaccessible part of the roof of his adopted home. Gef has offered very other proof of himself except the one which is essential for securing a verdict from a common-sense jury. So long as he remains shy, and is content to supply no more than equivocal tokens of his presence, so long must he remain of greater interest to the student of psychology than to the student of the supernatural. Under these conditions it is certain that "doubters" will abound, and that the faithful themselves will be able to do little more than acclaim Gef, with all his wit, malice and tomfoolery, as

VOX ET PRAETEREA NIHIL

(A Voice and Nothing More.)

APPENDIX A

CHRONOLOGICAL RECORD OF GEF'S ACTIVITIES, 1931-1935

1931

September. Gef begins to haunt Doarlish Cashen, and learns to speak. The news gets into the papers and the 'spook' of Glen Maye becomes a nine days' wonder. Doarlish Cashen is frequently visited by curious sightseers.

November. Mrs. Irving being away from home, Irving and Voirrey are roused from sleep late at night by a terrific scream, which the former attributes to Gef having taken and eaten some rat-poison which had been spread on bread and placed on top of Gef's 'sanctum'. The screams continued without stopping for twenty minutes, sounding like 'the screams of a pig when having a horseshoe nail put through the tip of his snout'. Subsequently Irving removed some of the match-boarding on the ceiling, and Voirrey climbed up through the aperture and made a thorough examination, but found nothing. On another occasion about the same time, when the whole family was at home, Gef sighed and moaned for thirty minutes without ceasing, and afterwards explained: 'I did it for devilment.' His favourite expression at this period was: 'I am a ghost in the form of a weasel, and I'll haunt you.'

December. Gef takes up a menacing attitude towards Voirrey, threatening her and throwing stones at her. The Irvings therefore decide to remove her bed into their own room. While they are doing this Gef, behind the panelling, screams and storms at them, thumping the panel with great violence. After the removal he screams out: 'I'll follow her, wherever you move her.' But after some months Gef recovers his temper, becomes more friendly, and promises: 'You can let Voirrey go back to her own room. I won't hurt any of you.'

December. During the absence of Mrs. Irving from home, Irving goes down to the local school to meet Voirrey, and fetch her home. Leaving Voirrey outside at play, he enters the schoolhouse and converses with the mistress, Miss Creer, chiefly about Gef. On leaving the school with Voirrey, while proceeding home up the glen after dark, Irving hears Gef's voice calling out: 'What did you tell Miss Creer about us?'

1931-1932

December to January. Gef spends time every day watching men at work on local road repairs, and reporting to Irving what they talked about. Upon one occasion a workman threw away a piece of bread, and later saw it moving towards the hedge apparently of its own accord. It is suggested that Gef (invisible) was carrying it off.

1932

February 12th. Miss Florence Milburn, of Peel, writes to Harry Price asking him to investigate Gef.

February 22nd. Irving's first letter to Harry Price.

February 26-28th. Captain Macdonald pays his first visit to Doarlish Cashen. At 11.45 p.m., as he is leaving the farm to return to Glen Maye, he hears a shrill voice scream from indoors, which Irving declares to be Gef. Captain Macdonald returns to the farm-house and waits a further fifteen minutes, but hears no more. Next day, on the 27th (Mrs. Irving being away in Peel) at tea-time a needle is thrown from the panelling and strikes a teapot: plates and crockery are moved in the pantry; these movements are attributed by Irving to Gef. In the evening, after Mrs. Irving's return from Peel, she and

Voirrey go upstairs, while Captain Macdonald and Irving remain below in the sitting-room. A shrill voice is heard from the bedroom, presumed to be Gef's. After fifteen minutes Captain Macdonald calls out to Gef asking him to come down, and receives the reply: 'No, I don't mean to stay long, as I don't like you.' Captain Macdonald tries to surprise Gef by crawling upstairs, but slips on a broken stair and falls down with a clatter. The voice screams out: 'He is coming!' Nothing more is heard. Captain Macdonald is partly convinced of Gef's reality, but still has some doubts.

March 7th. Mr. Northwood of Liverpool, an old friend of Irving, visits Doarlish Cashen, arriving midday. Irving invokes Gef. Voirrey goes into back kitchen, and Gef's voice is heard saying: 'Go away, Voirrey.' Later Gef repeats an Italian prayer after Irving. At lunch, when all the party is together, Gef is heard behind the boards in the kitchen calling out: 'Charlie, Charlie, chuck, chuck, chuck!' Later Gef urges Mr. Northwood not to let his son Arthur come up to Doarlish Cashen as 'he doesn't believe'. Heavy thumps on the ceiling and panelling of kitchen follow, then squeals. Gef continues to speak up to about 3 p.m., accusing Mr. Northwood of being a 'doubter'. On the way down to Glen Maye, Mr. Northwood hears three screeches from behind the hedge, which Irving declares to emanate from Gef. At 3.40 Mr. Northwood reaches the high road and motors away, convinced of Gef's reality. A few days later Mr. Northwood visits Doadish Cashen again, in company with his son and some relations. They all hear Gef, but afterwards retract their belief in him, except Mr. Northwood and his son.

March 16th. Gef speaks to Irving while the latter is alone in the house.

March 1th. Voirrey sees Gef on the garden wall, and tries to take a snapshot of him, but he jumps down and disappears before she can do so. March 21st. Irving's first letter to Captain Macdonald: 'I have recently discovered it [Gef] to be an Indian mongoose, several of which were turned loose a mile away by a farmer curiously enough named Irvine, about the year 1911 or 1912.' About this time Gef for the first time accompanies Irving and Voirrey to Peel and back, hiding behind the hedge and barking and calling to them. April 8th. Gef wakes Irving at 5 a.m. complaining: 'Jim, Jim, I am sick', and Irving hears him vomit behind the panelling. Subsequently Gef vomits carrots under Irving's bed, explaining he had eaten them at a cottage at Ballaheg, eight miles distant. April 14th-16th. According to his own account, Gef is absent from home on a visit to a farmer named Brew at Close Lake Ramsey, nearly twenty miles away.

April 30th. Gef runs on the cross-beams supporting the roof, so giving the Irvings a fair view of him. According to Irving, 'he is light yellow in colour, long bushy tail (which is also light yellow) and the tail has a black or brown tuft at the extreme end, and there are also, we think, two or three tufts of this brown or black hair on his back. His front feet resemble the human hand, and he appears to have three or four fingers and a thumb.' Mrs. Irving strokes Gef's head, and feels his teeth with her fingers, still while he is on the cross-beam.

May 2nd. Irving buys Gef a ball to play with. Gef thanks him for it, runs on the beams at night, and shows his hands through the opening between the bedrooms. Gef runs on the beams, and is visible to the Irvings, every night from April 30th to May 7th.

May 8th-9th. Gef absent at Balla Mona, twelve miles away. On his return says he has been to a party, eaten some pie, drunk cream out of a crock, and broken an egg.

May 11. Mr. and Mrs. Crookall visit Doarlish Cashen. Between 8-45 and 12.45 p.m. Gef speaks to them continuously. May 12th. Gef takes Irving's fingers in his paws. Mrs. Irving feels Gef's teeth again.

May 13th. Gef finds a paint brush in a rabbit hole a mile away and brings it home. In the evening he throws several small articles into Irving's bedroom, in presence of him and Mrs. Irving.

May 14th. Gef brings home a pair of iron pincers from a farm a mile and a half away.

May 15th-18th. Gef absent from home at a farm at Ballafreer, ten miles away.

May 19th. Gef throws a small bell into the kitchen, saying that he had taken it off some harness in a stable at Shenvalla, three miles away.

May 21st-22nd. Gef absent at Ronaldshay, twelve miles away, where he saw an aeroplane and a tractor in a field.

May 24th. Gef brings home a second paint-brush, and sings 'Carolina Moon' and other songs.

May 25th. During Mrs. Irving's absence in Peel, while Irving is in bed and Voirrey milking goats outside, Gef throws a grass mat in Irving's bedroom up into the air. Also throws small bone stud into the kitchen, saying he had taken it out of a workman's coat at Glen Maye.

June 4th. Gef converses with Voirrey alone, particularly concerning horse and foals. Sings songs unknown to the Irvings.

June 5th. Gef kills a small rabbit and lays it down near the house.

June 6th. Mrs. Irving feeds Gef on the beams. Every evening Gef chases the rats out of the outbuildings, with Irving looking on, and kills two small rats in their holes.

June 7th. Gef 80 years old today.

June 9th. Irving hears Gef speak Russian and sing a line of a Manx hymn. Gef kills a rabbit, which Voirrey fetches home.

June 15th. Gef throws stones at a lady visitor whom he styles 'doubter', but misses her and strikes her husband who is walking beside her. Gef says if Irving's elder daughter Elsie comes he will go away, or not speak whilst she is present.

June 17th. Gef throws a halfpenny into Irving's bedroom after he has gone to bed. Says he found it two miles away, and carried it home in his mouth.

June 18th. Gef passes to Mrs. Irving on one of the bedroom beams a ball of darning-wool said to be taken out of the hall of a house over a mile away.

June 19th. At his own suggestion Gef takes 'a biscuit from Voirrey's hands.

August 3rd-5th. Gef absent from home at Ramsey Cattle Show. During this month Gef suffers from a bad cough.

August 9th-13th. Gef absent at Castletown Show.

August 13th. Gef returns home, taps and scrapes on the panelling, and tells Irving he is shy.

October 22nd. Irving goes down to meet Mrs. Irving at Glen Maye, on her way back from Peel. As they return up the path to Doarlish Cashen, Gef throws stones at Mrs. Irving's back, calling out: 'Maggie the witchwoman, the Zulu woman, the Algerian woman, the Honolulu woman.' He is very pleased to see her back.

October 23rd. Voirrey sees Gef behind the house at 4.15 p.m. At night Gef sings Spanish songs sung by Spanish Jews of Turkey-also one verse of a Welsh song taught him by Irving.

November 3rd. Gef helps Irving to find one of' his lambs which is missing. He finds it among the sheep belonging to one of his neighbours. Gef says he is interested in horses and foals. Tells Irving: 'A mongoose can speak if he is taught.'

November 12th. Irving thinks he catches a glimpse of Gef crossing the main road a mile from Doarlish Cashen, moving at a terrific pace. Later Gef says: 'Yes, Jim, it was me, but I did not intend you to see me.'

December 2nd. During the absence of Mrs. Irving from the house, Gef tells Irving of her movements.

December 5th. Up to date Gef has killed twenty-three rabbits, all but three of them on Irving's property.

December 12th-16th. Gef missing.

December 19th-24th. Gef missing again. On his return he says: 'I will have one of Captain Macdonald's chocolates, a nut, and a black paradise and a muck sweet.'

1933

January. Irving hears indirectly through an acquaintance that mongoose are said in India to be able to talk, and that they possess a human brain and are very shy.

February 16th. By this time Gef can repeat Arabic, Hebrew, and Manx phrases spoken by Irving, and can read print. Gef promises Voirrey he will let her snap him with a camera, and Irving that he will sit on his knee in the parlour (neither promise apparently fulfilled at the time).

October. Mrs. Irving visits Peel. On her return Gef tells her of a conversation that has taken place during her absence between Irving and a corn-dealer.

1934

End of March. While Irving is reading front page of Liverpool Daily Post Gef calls out: 'I see something.' Asked what, he replies: 'I see a name that makes me quaky, that makes me shake', and tells Irving to look in the obituary notices column, where he finds an announcement of the death of a man named Jeffery, with the name Jef in brackets following.

April 16th. Up to date Gef has killed forty-seven rabbits, mostly apparently strangled. He has been seen out of doors twice by Irving and once by Mrs. Irving. Inside the house he has only been seen on the cross-beams. Gef is learning the deaf and dumb language from Irving. He frequently visits the motor-bus depot at Peel, and reports to Irving gossip which he has picked up among the mechanics at the garage. He asks Irving: 'When are you going to write to Harry Macdonald?'

June 4th. Gef guesses that a letter has arrived at Doarlish Cashen from Captain Macdonald, though this has been kept secret from Voirrey.

June 7th. Gef is 82 today.

June 8th. Irving, accompanied by Mona, goes out to clip sheep at a distance from the house and out of sight. While this goes on, Gef tells Mrs. Irving, who is left at home with Voirrey, which particular sheep Irving is clipping.

June 10th. Gef finds eggs laid by Irving's ducks in various odd corners of the farmyard.

June 17th. Five middle-aged visitors, including two spiritualists from Chester, at Doarlish Cashen. The latter declare that both Voirrey and Mrs. Irving are highly psychic, and that Gef is a spirit. They are rather nonplussed when Irving tells them that Gef eats ordinary food and kills rabbits. They hear nothing from Gef, who afterwards pronounces one of them to have been a 'doubter'.

June 19th. Gef rouses the family at 7 a.m., tells the time (correctly), and thumps violently on the ceiling. When asked if he will speak to Captain Macdonald when the latter visits Doarlish Cashen; he replies: 'Captain Macdonald can come, but not Harry Price. He's got his doubting cap on.'

June 24th. Late at night Gef speaks for two hours without stopping. Names forty different ailments, and says: 'Hey, jim, I've got joint evil in my tail.' Laughs with satanic laughter.

July 9th. Gef whistles and halloes from an outhouse to Irving and Mrs. Irving in their kitchen. He repeats what Mrs. Irving is saying.

July 10th-14th. Gef silent. At 11 p.m. on the 14th Gef thumps several times on the panelling and calls out: 'Hello, everybody.' When Irving ignores this, Gef thumps the panelling just behind his head and says: 'You devil, you heard' me before! What about my chukko (food)?' Mrs. Irving then feeds Gef with biscuits and lean bacon. They hear him munching and talking at the same time. Gef declares he has been away at the aerodrome at Ronaldshay, and repeats the conversation of two pilots, Captain O. and Captain H., whom he had seen there. Says he slept at night in a straw stack under a Dutch barn.

July 20th. Two young visitors from Wavertree have tea at Doarlish Cashen. Gef refuses to speak, but performs penny trick, also shuts Voirrey into her bedroom by means of catch fastening on the outside of her door. After the visitors' departure Mrs. Irving scolds Gef for not talking to them, and ignores his plea for food. Gef thumps on the panelling, and after Voirrey has given him some biscuits, throws the crumbs in her face. In reply to Mrs. Irving's request to tell her what he is, Gef replies: 'Of course I know what I am, and you are not going to get to know, and you are only grigged because I won't tell you. I might let you see me some time, but thou wilt never get to know what I am.'

July 23rd. Gef says he is going to a garden fete at Kentraugh, ten miles away.

July 24th. Gef absent at Kentraugh.

July 25th. Gef returns, and hunts a rabbit intended as a peace offering for Mrs. Irving. Says he has a present for her, and throws two biscuits on her while in bed.

July 26th. Gef, in high glee, sings three verses of 'Ell an Vannin', then two Spanish and one Welsh verse, then says prayer in Hebrew and a sentence in Flemish.

July 28th. Gef calls for food, whispering: 'Hey, Jim, what about some grubbo? I'm hungry.' Mrs. Irving throws a couple of biscuits on to his 'sanctum', and Gef is heard groping for them with his bony fingers. He takes a matchbox from Mrs, Irving, strikes a light, finds his biscuit; blows out match, and throws box back into the Irvings' bedroom, afterwards giving a long chuckle.

July 29th. Four young ladies from Liverpool (three being schoolteachers, and one a niece of Mrs. Irving) visit Doarlish Cashen. Gef does not speak. Later in the day he tells Irving: 'I have had a feed up on the three fields on the mountain. I caught a young partridge. I will vomit it up, if you give me some ipec. wine.'

August 6th. Gef follows Irving to Peel and back, proving the fact to Irving by repeating the latter's conversation with various people.

August 10th. Gef offers to touch Irving's hand on the roof-beam, but actually strikes it a hard blow with his 'fist'. Subsequently laughs and claps his hands. In response to questions, declares he has been in Africa, and has seen the Sphinx and Great Pyramid. Does arithmetic sums propounded by Mrs. Irving. Admits that 'for years I could understand all that was said. I tried to talk, but couldn't, until you taught me.' Said he had seen Voirrey on the Peel bus seven times in a fortnight.

Summer. Gef asks Irving if he has any enemies, and offers to kill their lambs. Says: 'You don't know what mischief I could do if I was roused. I could kill you too if I wished, but I won't.'

October 25th. Gef expresses dislike of Harry Price. 'He's the man who puts the kybosh on the spirits.' In the course of conversation Gef refers to the Gresford Colliery Disaster, Einstein, and Sir Isaac Newton, and says: 'I'll split the atom.' He promises to give Irving an imprint of his hand.

November 2nd. Gef pushes about a chair weighing twelve pounds on his 'sanctum'. He says: 'I am a freak. I have hands and I have feet, and if you saw me you'd faint, you'd be petrified, mummified, turned into stone or a pillar of salt.' Denies that he is a spirit.

November 6th. When asked what he will do for Captain Macdonald if the latter visits Doarlish Cashen, Gef laughs for three or four minutes, and declares: 'I have a pain in my side with laughing.'

November 7th-8th. Gef absent from home till the evening of the 8th, when he announces his return by calling out: 'If you knew what I know, you'd know a hell of a lot.'

November 10th. Gef calls family at daybreak, and in reply to Irving's questions says: 'I am not a spirit. I am a little extra, extra clever mongoose.'

November 19th. Gef pushes about a heavy chair on his 'sanctum', and indulges in satanic laughter.

End of November. Gef promises to let Voirrey snap him on the garden hedge. About this time an African spiritualist and her friend visit Doarlish Cashen. Gef speaks and performs penny trick, but when asked to show himself says: 'No damned fear; you'll put me in a bottle!'

December 11th. Gef speaking indistinctly and as if far off.

The Irving Family at Doarlish Cashen.

December 18th. To date Gef has killed fifty-four rabbits, the last weighing four pounds. Gef has a bad cough.

December 21St. Gef kills his fifty-fifth rabbit as a birthday present for Irving.

December 23rd. When Irving proposes to take snapshot of Gef, the latter says: 'You'll spoil it.' When Mrs. Irving proposes the same, Gef says: 'You, you could not take a pet lion. I do not trust any of the three of you.' At night Gef insists that Irving shall tell true ghost stories.

December 27th. Gef talks at night for two hours, thumps on panelling, throws matches on Irving's bed, and sings 'Isle of Capri' – also the following poem entitled 'Home on the Range': '*Home, home on the hills Where the nannies and bill goats play, Where Geoffrey is heard all day like a bird, At the home on the range in the hills*'. Gef claims: 'I am the Holy Ghost.' Later, he makes a pencil sketch on paper of the outline of his hand and foot. When asked by Irving if he would talk for Captain Macdonald, replies: 'Captain Macdonald is very kind, but he expects too much. He wants to know the ins and outs of a peanut.'

1935
January 1st. Gef away from home at the bus depot, Peel.

January 4th . Gef describes incidents of his past life in India. 'Two natives had me, one a tall man with a green turban, the other a little man, deformed or a hunchback. I was on the table in the house, and I knocked something over. Whereupon one said to the other: "Comee, comee, Gommadah, Mongus, Mongus".

January 9th. Gef kills two rabbits in one morning. January 19th. Gef in high spirits and sings hymn, 'Jesus, my Saviour, on Calvary's tree'. Asks Irving who God is, and on his replying: 'I do not know',

216

replies: 'Jim the infidel.' Afterwards Gef sings six verses of 'The King of Love my Shepherd is'.

January 20th. Gef talks, laughs, and sings an Indian song with chorus: 'Lowkee trooloo sonjemara, son jemara.' Also gives imitations of the Indians with whom he formerly lived. Says name of man who brought him from Egypt to England was 'Holland'.

January 26th. Gef in high spirits, laughing, talking, and singing parodies of songs not known to the Irvings.

February 1st. Gef kills his sixtieth rabbit. At night raids the butter in the store cupboard. Says he has been at Peel, listening to the talk of the men at the bus depot.

February 9th. Gef says: 'I have three attractions. I follow Voirrey, Mam gives me food, and Jim answers my questions.' Also: 'I have three spirits, and their names are Foe, Faith, and Truth.' (A variation on this is: 'Foe, Fear, and Faith'.)

February 11th. Gef manipulates flash-lamp on his 'sanctum'.

February 14th. Gef asks Mrs. Irving to put her hands through the gap above the cross-beam separating the two bedrooms. When she does so, he first strokes and licks her fingers, then takes the first three fingers of her right hand and holds them tight.

February 15th. In spite of wild weather, Gef kills his sixty-first rabbit, as a present for Mrs. Irving.

February 20th-21st. Gef absent from home at Peel bus depot. Subsequently repeats conversations heard there.

March 20th. In response to request Gef pulls out some of his fur from his back and tail, and tells Mrs. Irving: 'Look in the ornament on the mantelshelf and you will see something frail.' Irving sends the hairs to Captain Macdonald for identification. Captain Macdonald sends them on to Harry Price.

March 27th-31st. Gef again absent in Peel, sleeping at night in Dr. Longson's greenhouse. On his return Gef asks if the fur has been examined and identified yet.

April 1st-5th. Gef away from home again, wandering. Promises to sit for his photo, but fails to do so, not considering bribe of biscuits offered by Mrs. Irving sufficient.

April 9th. Harry Price forwards specimens of Gef's hair to Professor Julian Huxley, who sends them on to Mr. F. Martin Duncan for examination.

April 11th. Gef follows Irving, Voirrey, and Mona on a visit they are paying to neighbouring farm one mile away.

April 14th. Voirrey tries unsuccessfully to photograph Gef on the haggart (stackyard) wall.

April 23rd. Mr. . Martin Duncan writes to Harry Price about Gef's hair: 'I am inclined to think that these hairs have probably been taken from a longish-haired dog or dogs.'

May 1st. Voirrey snaps Gef in the haggart, but in bad light.

May 6th. Irving sends Captain Macdonald more samples of Gef's fur, placed in the bowl on the kitchen shelf. Gef celebrates Jubilee Day by paying a visit to Rushen, ten miles away, to hear a wireless broadcast.

May 15th. Gef's talkativeness causes Mrs. Irving to say she wishes he would talk when Captain Macdonald comes. To this, Gef replies: 'He's damned well not going to get to know my inferior complex.'

May 16th. Gef tells Irving his (Irving's) hair is as matted as Dick Swiveller's in the Old Curiosity Shop.

May 20th-21st. Captain Macdonald's second visit to Doarlish Cashen. He arrives at 7 p.m. on the 20th. Hears nothing until Voirrey is sent out to feed hens, when a scream is heard outside, said to be Gef's voice. Captain Macdonald then finds house door has been fastened from outside – which is also attributed to Gef. After this Gef demonstrates the penny trick to Captain Macdonald in the porch. The first time Gef guesses wrongly, the second time correctly. On the 21st Captain Macdonald and Irving walk down from Glen Maye village to the sea-shore; on their return to Doarlish Cashen Mrs. Irving tells them Gef has repeated to her part of their conversation. Later, Voirrey having gone outside, Gef speaks to Captain Macdonald, Irving, and Mrs. Irving together in the sitting-room, saying: 'Plus fours. Oxford bags' an allusion to Captain Macdonald's dress. At midnight, when Captain Macdonald and Irving have left the farm and are eighty yards away, the voice of Gef is heard nearby calling out 'coo-ee'.

May 24th. Gef expresses fear that Harry Price will put the account of Captain Macdonald's visit into the newspapers.

June 3rd. Mr. F. Martin Duncan sends photomicrographs of Gef's hair, etc., to Harry Price. 'I f you will look at these carefully there is little doubt that the "Talking Mongoose" hairs originated on the body of a dog.'

June 7th. Gef celebrates his eighty-third birthday.

June 28th. Harry Price writes to Irving proposing to visit Doarlish Cashen.

June 29th. Upon the arrival of Harry Price's letter, Gef disappears as from 10.30 p.m.

July 2nd. Irving replies to Harry Price, saying: 'Upon no account let this item [i.e. Gef's disappearance] deter you from paying us a visit, as since we first knew of his existence (September 1931) he has frequently been missing, or not heard, for 1, 2, 3 days, on one occasion 12 days; but ultimately he has always returned to what he himself calls home.' Irving suggests Harry Price should bring a camera with him, gives directions how to reach Glen Maye, etc. Middle of July. Voirrey leaves the Isle of Man for the first time in her life to cross to the mainland and spend a week with a relative in Liverpool. Meanwhile Gef is still silent and presumably missing from Doarlish Cashen. Mrs. Irving, however, believes he has not gone for good, since she attributes to him the upsetting of a pan of water which she had left untended upon her kitchen stove.

July 30th. Gef is believed by Mrs. Irving to have given another token of his presence in the house by moving a scrap of paper inserted by her in one of the crannies of the ceiling overnight.

July 30th-August 1st. Visit of Harry Price and R. S. Lambert to Doarlish Cashen. They arrive at Glen Maye about 7 p.m. on July 30th, and after supper in Irving's company, climb up the hill to the farm, arriving about nine. They present Voirrey with a new camera, for taking snaps of Gef. They leave again at 12.30, without having heard Gef, and return to Glen Maye. Next morning, July 31st, they take Irving and Voirrey round the island in a motor-car, visiting Peel and Ramsey, and returning to Glen Maye at 1.30. In the afternoon they again visit Doarlish Cashen, where they remain till after midnight. They inspect the farm- house and outbuildings, take photographs and other tokens of Gef, and invoke Gef to come out of his hiding and manifest himself – all without result. Mr. and Mrs. Irving express great disappointment at this failure. Irving fears Gef must have met with an accident or with foul play.

August 1st. After making inquiries concerning Gef among the village folk at Glen Maye, Harry Price and R . S. Lambert return to Douglas and thence home without having seen or heard Gef. At midnight on the same day Gef, after a silence of four weeks and five days, suddenly announces his presence again at Doarlish Cashen, by throwing some object into the Irvings' bedroom, clapping his hands, and laughing like a maniac. His first words were: 'Well, I've come back!' He declares he has been all over the island, but was present at home during the visit of Messrs. Price and Lambert. When asked by Irving why he did not speak, he says that there was a 'doubter' present, indicating Mr. Lambert. He describes Mr. Price's personal appearance ('looking like a minister'), also a gold ring which he wore on the little finger of his left hand. He admits to having been the culprit who upset Mrs. Irving's pan of water in July, at a time when Voirrey was away in Liverpool and Irving himself in Peel.

August 2nd. Irving asks Mr. Price to send him some plasticine, in order that an impress may be secured of Gef's hands and feet. August 6th. Gef promises to make an impress of his hands and feet in clay.

August 10th. Gef talks for one and a half hours at night. He confesses to having been present on July 11th, when three Jewish gentlemen (a lawyer, a teacher, and a doctor) visited Doarlish Cashen, and to have followed two of them up the path and heard the name of 'Morris Schofield' used. He' also repeats certain alleged conversation between Harry Price and R. S. Lambert which he claims to have overheard while they were out of doors in the farmyard during their visit.

August 12th. Gef kills his sixty-eighth rabbit, which Irving finds lying warm and limp in a gorse-bush.

August 13th. Gef makes impress of his foot on plasticine left overnight upon his 'sanctum' by Irving. When asked how he had done it, he replies: 'I put my foot on it, and gave it a twist, but the stuff was hard as hell.' Gef reports more fragments of alleged conversation overheard by him between Harry Price and R. S. Lambert. Mr. Martin Duncan reports to Harry Price on samples of hair brought back from Mona : 'Your sample on examination is absolutely identical with the alleged "mongoose" hairs.'

August 14th. Imprint of Gef's feet received by Harry Price.

August 16th. Gef kills his seventieth rabbit, a black one. Irving sends Harry Price an impress of Gef's teeth upon plasticine, saying that he had to assure Gef it was not poisoned before he would consent to touch it. Irving also sends impress of Gef's hands in dough.

August 18th. Irving sends two negatives (and prints) of Gef, taken by Voirrey. 'Print No. 1 shows a form on the top of a sod hedge; at this point the hedge is (approx.) 5 ft. high. I examined the spot most carefully a few minutes ago, and there is nothing on the hedge to be seen now. I had no difficulty in locating the place without Voirrey's assistance, as the stones shown in the middle of the snap were an excellent indication. Voirrey was at hand and confirmed that it was at this spot where she stood when Gef appeared at the top of the hedge. He remained standing on all fours facing the camera, until she called out: 'Away with you!' when she said he disappeared over the back of the hedge out of her view. No. 2 snap was taken in another field, perhaps 150 yards away, and the black-looking object on the top of the hedge is again Gef, once more facing the camera. . . . This should help you to form some idea of Gef's size, which is something a little less than an ordinary ferret.'

August 20th. Irving sends Harry Price further spools of film containing snaps of Gef, etc., to be developed and printed.

September 3rd. Irving writes to R. S. Lambert: 'I will certainly be interested to read the account of your visit in *The Listener*, and that at some future date Gef's history and our experiences be made public; because, amazing as they are, they have the merit of being true in every detail, and knowing it to be so I could face the world.' Irving sends detailed description of Gef to enable artist's sketch of him to be drawn.

September 5th. Irving sends two more snaps of Gef, taken on September 3rd. One of these shows Gef broadside on, with tail in a straight line with the body. Voirrey said 'he was squatted down. I have examined the sod hedge, and there is no grass on it, or any object, as it was burnt down in 1933 and is almost dead level.' Irving refuses invitation from Harry Price to let Voirrey visit London for a holiday under the care of a lady acquaintance. Irving sends complete list of Hindustani words used by Gef in his various conversations.

September 9th. Shown first draft of artist's sketch of him, Gef declares: 'That's not like me. It's like a lama', and suggests alterations.

September 10th. Mr. Northwood of Liverpool writes to Harry Price and R. S. Lambert saying that he had visited Doarlish Cashen twice, and had heard enough amazing things to convince him that all Irving had said about Gef was true.

September 11th. Harry Price publishes account of Gef in *The Listener*.

September 13th. Irving writes of *The Listener* article that 'on the whole it is not unfair'. This morning for the first time he sees Gef 'full face' for a second; he describes the face as having a flattish appearance.

September 16th. Irving sends Harry Price and R. S. Lambert copies of an enlarged photo of Gef.

September 20th. Mr. Northwood sends R. S. Lambert full notes and account of his experiences at Doarlish Cashen in March 1932. These are published in *The Listener* of October 2nd.

September 26th. Mr. Northwood offers to come to London to give oral evidence on behalf of Gef.

October 2nd-3rd. Captain Macdonald's third visit to Doarlish Cashen. He arrives at 5.30 p.m., to hear that Gef has been talking loudly all day. However, no sign of Gef heard until 11 p.m., when Voirrey went up to bed. After 11.30 raps are heard, and Captain Macdonald secures the fastener on the outside of Voirrey's bedroom door. Gef's voice is then heard giving shrill screams, accompanied by knocks and bangs in all parts of the house, lasting fifteen minutes. Captain Macdonald goes up and finds Voirrey still in bed, with chair fallen off Gef's 'sanctum' on top of her. He re-fastens door and descends to kitchen. Gef whistles, bangs on panelling, and laughs. His voice comes down staircase, and the Captain tries to catch him with the aid of his flash-lamp, but fails. Gef calls out 'Spies', and adds: 'Someone outside your house poaching your rabbits.' Knocks and bangs repeated from all parts of the house. A t 3 a.m. small stones and gravel are thrown at the outside of the windows of the house. After this Gef makes no further sound until 7 a .m., when he calls out to the Captain to get up. Captain Macdonald then leaves Doarlish Cashen. Weather very bad during the whole of his visit.

October 3rd. After 10 p.m. Gef bangs on panelling and eats cream buns purchased by Macdonald in Peel the previous day. Asked by Irving where he was when he spoke to Captain Macdonald on the stairs, he replies: 'Part of the time I was on the second stair from the top, and afterwards I was on the second stair from the bottom. I was there when Captain Macdonald hurried to the bottom of the stairs with his flash-light. I flew upstairs like hell, forgot Voirrey's door was fastened, and I banged into it. I had to jump into your room. He nearly saw me.' Mr. J. Radcliffe, director of the *Isle of Man Examiner*, writes to *The Listener* to give account of his visit to Doarlish Cashen in 1932, and expresses scepticism about Gef.

October 14th. Mr. Northwood visits London, sees Harry Price and R. S: Lambert, and is cross-questioned by them at the University of London Council for Psychical Investigation Laboratory.

October 21st. Mr. Northwood's son in the Royal Artillery writes to R. S. Lambert to confirm his father's account of Gef, having also been present at Doarlish Cashen on March 7th 1932.

November l0th. Up to date Gef's total kill of rabbits is one hundred and eighteen.

APPENDIX B

CAPTAIN MACDONALD'S FIRST AND SECOND VISITS

Report By Captain Macdonald of His First Visit to Doarlish Cashen

Sunday, 28,2,31

Dear Mr. Price,

So sorry I have been unable to send you a telegram or letter, but the nearest telegraph office is at Peel, 4 miles away, and there was no mail out from Douglas after the 9 a.m. Saturday boat until tomorrow, Monday morning.

I duly reached Douglas at 3.15 p.m. Friday, and took the trail on to Peel, where I arrived at 5.8 p.m.

As I was wearing the small button-hole you gave me. I had no difficulty in finding Mr. Irving, who was standing at the platform.

He had a car ready to convey me to Glen Maye, (about four miles away.) but suggested that we should first call and see Miss Milburn, whom you will remember was the lady who first wrote you.

Miss Milburn greeted me most cordially, and in course of conversation said that she only hoped the animal would come out and talk to me as everyone was anxious to know more about it!!

After leaving there, we motored on to Glen Maye, Mr. Irving having informed me that his house was quite near to the small village of that name.

During the run, Mr. Irving told me that I could stay at the Waterfall Inn, as he regretted that he could not put me up – when I saw his house later I was also thankful that this was not possible.

On arriving at Glen Maye I left my bag and prepared for my walk to Mr. Irving's place, Doarlish Cashen.

After a difficult climb of 40 minutes up a slippery precipitous path, I came to the farmstead, a very bleak stone building with its plaster surface worn and cracked by the weather (roughly we climbed 600ft.).

The door was opened by Mrs. Irving, a tall, dark lady, and when my eyes got accustomed to the meager candle-light of the living-room, I saw the daughter Voirrey (13 years of age) sitting in the corner of the room.

It must have been 7.30 p.m. when I reached the house, and I was only so glad that you were not with me, as I am certain you could not have managed the climb up to the house, in parts dangerous, and very slippery due to streams of water running down the narrow path.

I sat in a corner of the living-room, and listened to Mr. and Mrs. Irving again giving me their story, more or less in agreement with what we already had been told.

They then showed me various cracks and holes in the woodwork of the room which the animal used (so they said) to see who was there.

We sat and talked until just about 11.45 p.m., and, as nothing had taken place, I suggested making my way back to Glen Maye, wondering how on earth I should find my way back, as the night was very dark, and incidentally the cold extreme.

I was somewhat relieved when Mr. Irving said he thought he had better pilot me home, so we put on our overcoats and set forth.

Just as I had shut the door of the house we heard a very shrill voice from inside scream out: 'Go away. Who is that man?' Mr. Irving gripped my arm and said: 'That's it.'

I heard the shrill voice continuing, but was unable to catch exactly what it was saying.

We remained outside for five minutes, but I was so cold that I told Mr. Irving that I must either go in again, or go on down the hill.

We decided to go in, so I stalked back, and quietly got in the room, when the voice at once ceased.

We again sat down for 15 minutes, but nothing happened, so decided to leave — I eventually reached here in the early hours of Saturday morning, after nearly falling headlong into the stream!

I was beginning to be rather tired and 'fed up', as I had not been to bed since Thursday night: however, I turned in at 3 a.m. and was up on Saturday morning by 9 a.m. so as to have a real good day at the farm.

I reached Mr. Irving's house at 10.30 a.m. and he greeted me. He said that the animal had been talking that morning, and had promised to speak to me in the evening, provided that I made a promise to give Voirrey a camera or gramophone!!

I was also informed that I had to sit in a recess in the room, as the animal said it had been looking at me the previous night and did not like me; again, it also said that it knew that I did not believe in it, so I would have to shout out in the early evening that I did believe in it, etc., etc.

Well, we hung about the house all day (Mrs. Irving having gone to Peel) and again I was asked to examine the house, etc., etc.

At 5.30 p.m. Mr. Irving suggested a cup of tea, so the daughter prepared some, and then we three sat down at the table.

While we were talking something was thrown from the panel behind Mr. Irving. It struck the teapot, or possibly a cup, and Mr. I. said: 'That's the animal.' We examined the cloth and found a large packing-case needle, which I picked up and gently threw at the teapot, when exactly the same noise was again made, Mr. I. saying that it constantly threw things at the family.

At 6.15 p.m. we heard plates and similar things being moved in the small scullery. No one was there. A little later, again the same noise, and again no one there, but we found a little stream of water running from a small hole in the wall, which Mr. I. said was the animal performing its natural functions. I saw no sign of rats, or mice, but Mr. I. said that there were plenty of weasels about.

At 7.30 Mrs., I. returned from Peel, and was astonished to hear that the animal had not spoken, in view of its morning promise.

At 7.45 p.m. Mr. I. said to his wife: 'Go upstairs and see if you can make the creature begin', adding to me: 'If we can get him to start upstairs he will then come into this room.' So upstairs went Mrs. and Miss I. to the bedroom over our room.

In about 3 minutes there was a shrill scream, Mr. I. saying: 'There it is'; then Mrs. I. said: 'No, come on and talk', whereupon a very shrill voice started talking in the bedroom, and kept on talking to Mrs. I. for 15 minutes. I then shouted that, as I believed in the animal, would it come down. I received a shrill reply: 'No, I don't mean to stay long as I don't like you.'

However, the shrill, piping voice kept on talking, but in view of the fact that the voice came from upstairs, where both Mrs. and Miss were, it was not of much value.

I then quietly crawled up the dark staircase but by sheer bad luck, and owing to one of the stairs being broken, I slipped and fell, making a terrible noise – the result being that the shrill voice screamed: 'He is coming!'

Nothing more at all happened, and I stayed there till nearly midnight and got to bed 1 a.m. Sunday.

I am looking forward to a square meal sometime today, Sunday.

I don't quite know what I really think, as the attitude of the Irvings has rather defeated me. Mr. Irving appears to be a perfectly genuine man and quite above the Manx farming class. I have seen him again this morning, and he again assures me that the animal has had a lengthy talk with him early this morning, and asked for some bread and milk.

I can tell you a good deal more, but this will give you a rough idea of what has taken place.

Please excuse scribble, so little time to get this done.

Sincerely,

    (Signed) M. A. MACDONALD

Waterfall Hotel,

    Glen Maye, Isle of Man

Report By Mr. Irving of Captain Macdonald's Second Visit to Doarlish Cashen With Corroborative Comments By Captain Macdonald

                                         Friday, May 24th 1935

Dear Captain Macdonald,

I will confine this letter to those incidents you experienced on your visit to Doarlish Cashen, 20th to 23rd May, and in the order in which they occurred and trust you will find them in accord with your own recollection of what took place. You arrived at the house about 7.00 p.m., and in a few moments we all sat down to tea, and naturally the conversation turned to Gef, and I asked my wife if she had heard him during · the time I was away meeting you at Ronaldsway. She said she had not heard him since morning, and that she was not surprised, as he (Gef) had declared he was going to Ronaldsway, but, added my wife: 'I am sure he is about here now.'

We waited patiently for quite a long time, but, with the exception of 2 or 3 undefinable noises in the house, and which you also said you heard, there was no sign of Gef, and, as the evening was getting on, it was necessary for Voirrey to leave the house to feed 2 or 3 sitting hens in the stackyard, 90 to 100 feet away from the house.

She was absent only a few minutes, but during that time we, inside the house, yourself included, heard Gef (outside) scream, but could not distinguish the word (or words), as the house walls being 2 ft. 6 in. thick, and the windows not opening, make the house almost sound-proof. In a minute Voirrey entered the house and asked had we heard Gef, as he had screamed the one word 'Sapphire'. This use of the word puzzled us, until, without speaking you lifted your hand off the table and showed a ring on your finger. You then took the ring off, and allowed us to see it, and I then saw it was a sapphire.

After your departure that night Gef was asked how he knew. He answered: 'I saw the ring.' Questioned as to how he knew it was a sapphire, answered: 'Never mind how I know, I know.' And that was all we could get out of him.

[Note by Captain Macdonald. Prior to the coins, I must mention that Mr. and Mrs. Irving and self were sitting in the living-room talking, whilst the daughter was out attending to the goats. There is a small lobby between the outside door of the house and the living-room, and a second door from the lobby (to exclude draughts). On rare occasions this latter door is locked by padlock and hasp should the family be away, so the hasp is fitted on the outside of the door. For some reason I wanted to have a look outside, and on turning the handle of the door found I was unable to get out. We had to wait until the daughter returned before we could get out, and she found the hasp had been placed over the loop. The Irvings said: 'That's Gef', so I suggested to Mr. Irving that as we were then all in the house that I should shut the door. This I did, having first examined the hasp to see if possibly it could get hung up in the loop. I then banged the door to many times, but found that the hasp, due to age and being loose, always fell below the hoop. Within the two minutes we again found the door locked and with difficulty forced it open. I then shouted: 'Did you do that, Gef?' and although I heard an answer, could not say exactly what it was, but Mr. Irving said that he heard it and it was that Gef said: 'I did that.' On examining the lobby, Mr. Irving showed me a hole near the rafters and he said that no doubt Gef came through same to put the hasp on the loop, as he often used that particular hole, and sometimes took food if placed there.]

After this came the demonstration of the coins (head or tail). You went into the porch, and I showed you where to place a penny, and you were to satisfy yourself that we three (self, wife, and Voirrey) were so placed in our living-room that it would be an absolute impossibility for any of us to see the coin. The first time Gef named the coin wrongly. I was angry, and insisted that he must tell correctly, and he did so, and I then asked Gef to call the next toss, and to this request Gef called out: 'Hanky panky work; he has not touched the coin.' I questioned you and you said you had not touched the coin, but had left it lying where it was. You then tossed the coin again, and Gef once more told correctly. The evening was now far advanced and as Gef would do no more, you left the house for the hotel. After you had left, my wife was vexed with Gef for keeping us so long without speaking, and he pleaded: 'I was tired. I had to walk home from Ronaldsway' (12 miles or more from here).

I now come to Tuesday (May 21st). I met you leaving Peel, and we came back to the Waterfall Hotel and had lunch together. We afterwards walked past the falls, and in due time reached the shore, stayed a while and came back to the hotel, and had afternoon tea, and we then proceeded to Doarlish Cashen, arriving there about 6.30 p.m.

You were told by my wife that Gef had not been heard since breakfast and that she was sure he had followed me down to Glen Maye, and this he had done; as you will recollect, later on my wife was able to say the subject-matter we had conversed about whilst walking past the falls to the beach.

[Note by Captain Macdonald. On Tuesday, May 21st, Mr. Irving had lunch with me at the Waterfall Hotel, Glen Maye. I asked him what he would drink with this meal, and he replied that 'a glass of Manx beer will suit me well'. After lunch we walked down to the beach, and, as I was so impressed with the beauty of the glen path down to the sea, remarked to Mr. Irving that he should bring his wife down as everything was looking so perfect. His reply to this was: 'Well, I'm afraid she has no suitable shoes.' Shortly after, on reaching the shore, I said to Mr. Irving that I felt sure Gef was with us. I just had that presentiment, and it was so strange that I wanted to know if he shared my opinion. His reply was: 'That's more than likely, as he follows me to Peel (a good 4 miles away) so often.' Just before leaving I picked a flower and put it in the button-hole of my jacket, and we then strolled back up the Glen towards the village en route for Doarlish Cashen. On our arrival at Doarlish Cashen, Mrs. Irving said to me: 'Gef has been with you. He saw "Pots" [Gef's nickname for Irving] have beer for lunch and he has told me of your conversation on the shore about my lack of shoes, and he saw you pick a daisy from the bank near the sea.' Mrs. Irving added: 'I wanted to tell you this the moment you arrived, so that you would be certain that my husband could not possibly have told me.']

After this you inquired of my wife if Gef were about now, and was it not too early. She answered: 'No. It is not too early for him. He is in the house now. I feel sure he is.'

Still no sign of Gef, and as the time was going, Voirrey went to the stackyard to feed the sitting hens, leaving we 3 alone in the living-room, and then came the demonstration that only happens once in a very long time. Quite unexpectedly Gef spoke as follows: 'Plus fours, Oxford bags', an allusion to your attire.

When he said these words the voice was a few feet away, and behind the wainscot, my wife and self were both within a few feet from you, and in full view also, and Voirrey at this moment (and this is important) was 100 feet away from the house, out of sight and out of sound in the stackyard, and I at once asked you to come to the window and see for yourself, and in 2 or 3 seconds she appeared at the entrance to the stackyard, coming towards the house.

I will now skip over one or two other incidents, and deal with what I consider an important one, and the one which interested you most. It was midnight when you and I left the house to return to your hotel, leaving my wife and Voirrey in the house.

We had reached a point (80 paces away…I stepped it) when Gef called out 'coo-ee' to us. You at once recognized Gef's voice (once heard, never forgotten), and you said: 'That's Gef. That's Gef, and he is quite close to us.' I dissented, and thought he was some distance away, but, later on, I found you were quite correct – he was actually 10 feet away, as Gef later told me he was at the gap when he called to us.

Now what I wish to impress upon you is this. In these 2 experiences you have had what no one else has had (excepting ourselves), that is, you heard him speak in the house whilst my daughter was out of the house (100 feet away), and he spoke to us both outside the house and when my daughter was in the house. Many people have heard Gef speak in the house whilst Voirrey was not in, but no one has heard him speak outside the house and Voirrey inside, so that your dual experiences in this respect are absolutely 'unique', and you have been very fortunate.

So rarely has the foregoing happened even to us, ourselves, that I make special note of it in my diary now in your possession.

I will now deal with one of the skipped incidents, that of the whispering. My wife and Voirrey stood at the far end of the pantry, you and I in the deep window recess in our living-room, 30 feet from them; and, whispering in the faintest possible voice, not to be heard (by a human) more than 2 feet away, you asked: 'What flower is this?' Gef called out at once: 'A sea flower.' Actually the sea-pink you picked at Glen Maye beach and it was in the button-hole of your coat.

This was proof positive that Gef had followed us both to the beach and had seen you pluck the flower.

(Signed) Jas. T. Irving

APPENDIX C

CROSS-EXAMINATION OF MR. NORTHWOOD

Verbatim report of conversation between Harry Price, R. S. Lambert, and Mr. Northwood at the o.ffices of the University of London Council for Psychical Investigation on Monday, 14th October 1935

Northwood: 'Ask any questions you like.'

Lambert: 'One of the points is whether you think it at all likely that Voirrey can ventriloquize?'

Northwood: 'That is a farcical notion. Voirrey is only a child, and has no knowledge of ventriloquism. The family is too honest to adopt such a subterfuge. There might be a curious alliance of thought, or something extraordinary in Voirrey, but I could not see anything suspicious. Gef is very fond of the child.'

Lambert: 'Is Voirrey fond of Gef?'

Northwood: 'That I cannot tell. She is quiet and reserved, but I cannot tell. She has to be drawn out. The child has got more of the character of her mother, and she would not deceive any one. Irving sent me a note to come and see Gef, and I went. Mrs. Irving was honestly delighted that I heard the animal. As regards Voirrey I cannot say.'

Lambert: 'How many times have you heard Gef?'

Northwood: 'Twice. In March 1932, and then again a few days later. My sisters-in-law and a little girl (the elder sister-in-law's girl) heard Gef. Also my son. He heard it when I heard Gef the first time, not the second.'

Lambert: 'Your son was not wholly convinced?'

Northwood: 'He wavered a little. He joined the Army, and if you want to see him, he would tell you all about his experience. I could tell him to come and see you. He is the type of lad who sees things, but forgets them, as he does not like to be laughed at. I could tell him to come to you.'

Price: 'So your son was impressed at first, but afterwards wavered?'

Northwood: 'Yes, he was impressed, but he laughed about it.'

Lambert: 'You have not been to Doarlish Cashen since?'

Northwood: 'No, I have not. I was there in 1932, and then in 1934. I saw Irving, but not at Doarlish Cashen. He came to Peel. I was over there three or four times in 1932, and I learned from Irving many extraordinary things. He spoke for hours and hours on end. He seems obsessed with the thing.'

Lambert: 'Are there any people in the neighbourhood who believe in Gef?'

Northwood: 'My two nieces heard it.'

Lambert: 'I mean anybody living near the farm.'

Northwood: 'Not that I know of.'

Lambert: 'When we were there, no one seemed to stand by the story.'

Northwood: 'That is the fault. A fellow would rather keep it to himself, and not make a fool of himself.'

Lambert: 'Tell us about your second visit.'

Northwood: "I went with my sister-in-law. We heard the animal screaming and shouting out. But I cannot quite remember, as I did not take any notes, or put anything down.'

Lambert: 'Then you went a few weeks later?'

Northwood: 'No, a few days later. I told several people about it. They believed me, because I am well known on the island. I was convinced it was a physical phenomenon. This was in 1932. But I didn't keep a record. Gef said the name of my sister-in-law's child, and said she had a powder-puff in her bag.'

Price: 'Voirrey was aware of those facts which Gef put forward, about the powder-puff, etc.?'

Northwood: 'Yes, she was there in the room at the time.'

Lambert: 'What convinces you that it was not Voirrey or Irving speaking?'

Northwood: 'I see what you mean. But how can you explain the voice coming from a hole in the porch, really from the porch, when we were in the kitchen, and also in the sitting-room? The voice came very loudly: "Charlie". It was louder than that.'

Lambert: 'What sort of voice?'

Northwood: 'Like a woman's voice; like a girl's voice of about fifteen or sixteen – a striking, penetrating voice; high. The voice was malevolent and full of venom. It said: "Doubter, Doubter."'

Price: 'That house is like a speaking-tube with all that panelling.'

Northwood: 'Yes, that is right. But the voice came from the sitting-room, high and shrill. Not like an ordinary girl's voice. Like a girl of fifteen, but falsetto. It seemed to grow in volume all the time. It was absolutely loud at the end. It talked a lot, but that is some of Irving's talk. Gef repeats what Irving says.'

Lambert: 'Did you ever hear the voice outside?'

Northwood: 'I only heard it outside when I was going down the road to Peel to telephone. I heard a squeak three times. Irving said to me: "That's it!" The child was with me then; she was following Irving and me.'

Price: 'Do you know the exact position of Irving and Voirrey in regard to yourself walking down the path, as it is very narrow, and two cannot walk abreast.'

Northwood: 'Yes, that's true. I cannot remember, but both were close to me.'

Price: 'If Voirrey was behind you, she could have done the "voice".'

Northwood: 'I see what you mean, but the child couldn't deceive. I'd be glad to give you any doubts which I may have, but I haven't any. Admittedly Gef is friendly with Voirrey.'

Lambert: 'It is very unlikely to be ventriloquism.'

Price: 'Assuming Voirrey is the culprit, consciously or unconsciously, no one except a madman could live in the house for four years without knowing it.'

Northwood: 'That's right. But I do not think she is. Irving is very sincere about it all.'

Lambert: 'It is odd that Gef wouldn't appear when we went.'

Northwood: 'Yes, it is.'

Price: 'It is odd, too that Gef has often mentioned my name when talking to the Irvings, e.g. "Pnce is a doubter", "Price puts the kybosh on spirits" etc. He seemed rather afraid of me long before I arrived on the scene. Why was Gef afraid?'

.Northwood: 'He may have suspected you. But then why did Gef ask the University Council to investigate if he was afraid?'

Price: 'But neither he nor Mr. Irving asked me to investigate. I wrote and asked them.'

Lambert: 'We went over there but did not see Gef. He had not been photographed up till that time. Mr. Price very kindly gave Voirrey a camera, and she has taken certain pictures which are odd; you can see something like a large squirrel which, Irving says, is Gef. It is half hidden in the grass. Certainly, Mr. Price was very kind to both Mr. and Mrs. Irving, so I am sure they would be willing to help in any way to make Gef speak.'

Price: 'Yes, Irving asked me to stay in the house during my visit, but this was impossible, when it was arranged that Mr. Lambert should go with me."

Lambert: 'Have you heard from Irving lately, Mr. Northwood?'

Northwood: 'I wrote and told him about my being in correspondence with you. He replied: "I have today seen the animal face to face for the first time. You have heard it speak more than anyone else." I have never been to a spiritualist meeting in my life, as I do not believe in these things.'

Lambert: 'What do you think Gef is?'

Northwood: 'I think it is some extraordinary animal which has developed the power of speech by some extraordinary process.'

Lambert: 'It is intelligent.'

Northwood: 'Yes. The way it gets the rabbits, and finds the lost sheep. Once, for a Christmas present for Irving, it put a sixpence on the table. It had probably pinched it out of some workman's pocket.'

Lambert: 'Irving told us a story about the rabbits. He said that Voirrey and Mona (the dog) had developed a method of catching the rabbits. Voirrey would tell Mona to point a rabbit, which became mesmerized, and Voirrey would creep round behind the rabbit and knock it on the head with a stick or something, and would thus kill it. The rabbit would be too mesmerized to move.'

Northwood: 'Irving has never told me that. He said that Voirrey had developed some power, and that the child could get more rabbits than anyone else.'

Price: 'How do you account for our expert saying that the specimens of hair which Irving sent as being Gef's hair are those from a collie dog?'

Northwood: 'Yes. I read it in your article. Of course there are inconsistencies.'

Lambert: 'The only explanation is that Gef was playing a joke on them and took Mona's hair and said it was his own.'

Northwood: 'Yes. I suppose so.'

Price: 'Perhaps you would like to see the imprints which Gef has made.'

Northwood: 'Yes. I should like to see them.'

(Here, Mr. Price showed   Mr. Northwood imprints.)

Price: 'It seems extraordinary that the large one and the small one should come from the same animal.'

Northwood: 'Yes. I should say they were rather big for a mongoose. I have an aunt in Douglas who has a stuffed mongoose in a glass case. I looked at its claws, and they are quite different from these imprints. Irving says Gef's claws are something like a human being's hand.'

Price: 'What pressure do you think would be necessary to stamp those imprints in plasticine? Gef is only two pounds in weight, and I should think more pressure than that would be required to imprint those in the plasticine.'

Northwood: 'Yes. These imprints seem to me much larger than what I would expect. What would you suggest about a dictaphone or microphone to record Gef's voice?'

Price: 'The trouble is that there is no electricity there. There are, so far as I know, no clockwork dicta phones to be had.'

Northwood: 'But there are dictaphones in offices all over the place.'

Price: 'Yes, but they have a good supply of electricity.'

Northwood: 'Isn't it possible to run one off a battery?'

Lambert: 'Of course it could be done by taking a van and all the necessary apparatus.'

Price: 'Oh, yes. It would be possible by making one's own electricity.'

Lambert: 'A wire would have to be run across the moors to the cottage.'

Price: 'Not necessarily. A van could get up to the cottage if it had tractor wheels.'

Lambert: 'I don't think so.'

Price: 'Yes, a tractor could get across that rough and barren land.'

Lambert: 'In any case, the trouble is that Gef might not speak after all the preparation.'

Northwood: 'The thing to do would be to switch on when Gef was speaking.'

Lambert: 'But Gef is so suspicious. He would think we were trying to put him in a bottle, or something.'

Price: 'I can think of a much easier way. Those recording gramophone disks.'

Northwood: 'Yes, that was what I was thinking. If such a thing could be managed it would go all over the world.'

Price: 'Irving could get it on one of those disks.'

Lambert: 'Except that it is an expensive job.'

Price: 'No, I don't think so. They are only about half a crown each.'

Lambert: 'Not the good ones.'

Price: 'I do not think they are so bad.'

Northwood: 'I wouldn't mind spending a hundred or two myself to see the whole thing through.'

Lambert: 'But recording a voice does not prove Gef; we want to hear Gef himself.'

Northwood: 'As you explained, what you want to see is to have Gef in front of you, speaking to you.'

Price: 'No. What we want is to have the animal speaking to us when all the three are in front of us. That would be proof.'

Northwood: 'Yes, that's right. It is necessary to think out means of doing this.'

Lambert: 'Could you persuade Irving? He has gone two-thirds of the way with indirect evidence. The other third of direct evidence is lacking. It is this third which is the missing link. You see, we want to establish facts.'

Northwood: 'I quite see your point of view. But that blessed animal seems to know what you are about.'

Lambert: 'But why won't he prove himself to us?'

Northwood: 'There you are! Irving told the animal that he was going to bring a dictaphone to record his voice, but Gef refused to speak into a dictaphone.'

Price: 'Why? He has recorded his footprints, given specimens of his hair, etc., but won't record his voice.'

Northwood: 'There is a certain amount of childishness about Gef. Irving has told me some very extraordinary things about the animal.'

Price: 'Well, if it is eighty-three years old, it must have learnt a lot by now.'

Northwood: 'Yes, and it tells things beyond my and Irving's knowledge.'

Price: 'But surely Gef has never said anything which has been above the knowledge or mentality of Voirrey or Irving?'

Northwood: 'No. I suppose not. Gef has picked up things from the Irvings.'

Lambert: 'It is a great pity, as Gef cannot be, so to speak, "turned on to order". Gef will not come and go just as you like.'

Northwood: 'I quite see all the difficulties.'

Lambert: 'From the point of view of science, it is very interesting.'

Northwood: 'It is absolutely unique. I can vouch for it. You can ask me any questions you like.'

Lambert: 'You think it is quite impossible for Voirrey to do the talking?'   ·

Northwood: 'Yes. From my own knowledge it is impossible for Voirrey to do it.'

Price: 'When you heard Gef speak, Irving and Voirrey were there all the time and you watched Voirrey and didn't see her mouth move?'

Northwood: 'Yes, I think so. The only thing I could see was that the animal was attracted to Voirrey. If it is very late, Irving tells her to go upstairs.'

Price: 'Another question. Have you seen Voirrey and Irving close to you, and have you watched Voirrey when the animal was talking?'

Northwood: 'Yes, at lunch. Gef spoke from behind the boards. Voirrey was in the kitchen when Gef spoke to my sister-in-law.'

Price: 'That is not quite the same thing. It is quite obvious that I couldn't make my voice come from the office, while you and Mr. Lambert were watching me.'

Northwood: 'That is true. Ventriloquists use a doll in order to misdirect the audience. But Irving hasn't got those things.'

Lambert: 'There is a doubt about the animal talking. Is the voice heard at one corner and then at another?'

Northwood: 'Yes, but what about the thumping? I have heard it. Loud thumps come on the far side of the house, then in the kitchen, then somewhere else.'

Lambert: 'Have you heard it by the stairs?'

Northwood: 'Not on the boxing of the stairs. Over the back of the kitchen. Voirrey was not in my presence then. Then Gef shouted out: "Vanished." Irving calls that Gef's magic.'

APPENDIX D

GEF AS A FAMILIAR

GEF does not fit into any of the usual categories of abnormal phenomena recognized by psychical research. He possesses an animal form, the power of speech, and intelligence – three characteristics not found together in any ordinary case of present day haunting. But if Gef had appeared three hundred years ago there would have been absolutely no difficulty in saying what he was. Matthew Hopkins, the Witchfinder-General, would have instantly classified him among the imps, or familiars, nourished and used by the unfortunate creatures he was convicting of witchcraft. Mr. C. L'Estrange Ewen in **Witchcraft and Demonianism** (1933) gives exhaustive particulars of the various kinds of familiars, and of their ways of behaviour. It is astonishing to find Gef anticipated in so many ways. Almost all domestic or household animals, and many wild animals and insects, were used as familiars; among these the squirrel, the ferret, the polecat, and the rabbit were common. Joan Prentice of Sible Hedingham (Essex) confessed in 1589 that six years previously the Devil had appeared to her in the form of a dun-coloured ferret with fiery eyes, which demanded her soul. The ferret's name was Bidd, and it used to suck blood from the forefinger of her left hand-reminding us of Gef's achievement in drawing blood from the hand of Mrs. Irving. Elizabeth Bennet of St. Osyth (Essex), who was hanged in 1581, was also accused by her fellow-witches of cherishing a ferret among her other familiars. John Stearne, who was Matthew Hopkins' assistant, testified in 1644 that Elizabeth Clarke called up before his eyes seven or eight of her familiars, among whom was a ferret – though Hopkins himself described it as a fulmer, or polecat. In a Tewkesbury case (described in 1693) a farmer speared with a fork a witch in the form of a polecat which was attacking his pigs. Again, Philippa Munnings of Hartest (Suffolk) was accused and acquitted of witchcraft in 1693; but no fewer than nine witnesses at her trial swore that she had entertained an evil spirit in the likeness of a polecat.

These familiars sometimes lived in the cracks of the walls of their owner's cottages; they were treated like ordinary domestic pets, 'as one of the household', and fed on bread, cheese, beer, water, milk, wheat, oats, barley, and sometimes chickens. They were often capable of speech and spoke good English, but generally in a hollow voice, like the cat of Elizabeth Francis (1566). In 1586, Joan Cason of Faversham was accused of possessing 'a little thing like a rat (but more reddish) having a broad tail', which one heard 'cry in the wall like a cricket', saying: 'Go to, go to!' Sometimes the speech of the familiars was hard to understand. Though intelligent, they were capable of mistakes and misunderstandings, as well as of breaking their promises. They frequently fetched victuals for their hosts, sometimes found lost objects (such as purses), and were kept employed on errands, generally harmful, to other folk and their property. Occasionally familiars lived to a great age – forty or sixty yrs. They were usually given names by their owners, but sometimes announced their own.

All these points can be paralleled in the history of Gef and in addition we have a final point of general similarity, interesting to anthropologists, between the economic environment of the seventeenth-century familiar and that of his twentieth-century descendant. Three hundred years ago the English countryside was dotted with farmsteads like Doarlish Cashen – isolated from society and yielding their occupiers but a scanty livelihood. During the monotony of the long, dark winters of those days what distorted visions and fantasies may not have arisen, what strange schemes of bizarre entertainment not been engendered in the imagination! Out of a mere exhibitionism women used to confess to the unpleasant but ludicrous habits of witchcraft, knowing perfectly well that such confession would lead them to the gallows. Nowadays witchcraft is no more a punishable offence, but neither is it a profitable pursuit. Nor do we any longer meet with familiars. But may not ghosts have ghosts, who in out-of-the-way places carry on their attenuated existence in the cracks of old foundations and behind the chinks of draughty partitions?

A REFLECTION ON GEF

By Tim R. Swartz

"The Haunting at Cashen's Gap" was published in 1936. However, despite the earlier infatuation with Gef, provoked by newspaper accounts, *"The Haunting at Cashen's Gap"* quickly sank into oblivion after selling less than 500 copies. In their book, Harry Price and R.S. Lambert handle Irving's (and others) accounts of Gef in a straightforward fashion, offering up no personal conclusions on the case. In the introduction, the author's state: "To believers it will represent a proof of miracle; to skeptics a lesson in the laws of evidence. Some will cast it nonsense from first to last; others will admit it to be at least as good as most ghost stories. Throughout we have sought to avoid mere credulity on the one hand and prejudiced skepticism on the other."

After the book was published, Price would later say that he thought that Gef was a hoax, not a hoax for profit, but a "psychological hoax." Price reflected that the Irving's, who had found themselves isolated, not only in location, but also isolated in their lives after seeing their former, more affluent, existence slowly stripped away. Price suggested that the family suffered from some kind of shared delusion of a talking animal in their house. A delusion that perhaps had been started by Voirrey as a joke, but then escalated beyond her control when Jim Irving found that Gef was a way for him to regain some of the thwarted ambitions and importance in his life that he imagined he deserved.

Price's viewpoint makes a certain amount of sense. Residents of Man during the time of Gef thought the whole "Dalby Spook" affair was a hoax, brought about by Mrs. Irving and Voirrey who had hoped that Gef would scare Mr. Irving enough to sell the farm and move back to Liverpool. Nevertheless, if this was true, they utterly failed as Jim Irving became obsessed with Gef and remained at Doarlish Cashen until he died in 1940.

Nandor Fodor eventually came up with a somewhat similar viewpoint as Price. But rather than Gef being entirely the product of a "combined delusion," he thought that there was much more to Gef then that. When Fodor spent a week with the Irving's in 1936, he noted "The air, 750 feet above sea level, is remarkably pure and invigorating; its water is excellent. The members of the Irving family are very healthy. They are normal apparently in every respect." (Nandor Fodor, "*Haunted People*," page 192). Fodor speculated that perhaps Gef was a paranormal creation, an external manifestation of the inner turmoil within the minds of the family members (perhaps a "Tulpa" or "thought form").

This idea that Gef was more than an "imaginary friend" with Freudian overtones came about because he had the ability to interact with others outside of the Irving household. One witness interviewed by Fodor was John Cowley, who was a mechanic at Peel. Cowley had heard that Gef was secretly riding the bus so he rigged up an electric trap under bus 81 in order to kill him. Cowley was quoted as saying: "It did not work. Nor the wire cage which I placed baited under the waiting room to stop the stealing of sandwiches. Mr. Irving told me where the electric trap was fixed. He said that Gef knew all about it. This animal, or whatever it is, knows a darn sight too much. He seems to hear what we talk in the bus-shed, behind closed doors, in the early morning hours, when no one is about."

Hoax?

It is easy on retrospect to declare the entire Gef affair as a hoax. So many years have passed and armchair skeptics are quick to dismiss everything outright without taking the time to thoroughly examine the information that is now available. Voirrey Irving is often suspected as being the hoaxer as often when Gef was talking and/or producing various physical activities, she was present. As mentioned earlier in this book, Voirrey was accused of being a ventriloquist with the ability to imitate animal noises. There is little doubt that Voirrey did hoax some of Gef's activities from time to time. Any examination of recorded poltergeist cases that involve children will show that this is a common occurrence, especially when the poltergeist is called upon to perform on demand and it doesn't.

If Voirrey was hoaxing Gef for the entire duration of the phenomena, her parents must have been the most clueless, unobservant and guileless parents in the history of parentdom. Anyone who has children is well aware of their tricks and deceptions...this is one of the special powers that parents have. They may be fooled occasionally, but they quickly learn to be on top of everything their child does and to, for the most part, be able to tell facts from fictions.

When Jim and Margaret Irving were involved with the Gef affair, they had not just fallen off the hay truck into the life of being parents. They had already raised two children to adulthood by the time Voirrey was born. At that point they should have been well aware of the troubles that children can, and do, cause, and be ready

257

to respond accordingly. One must also remember that both Jim and Margaret were parents in a time when children were to be seen and not heard. Jim Irving especially was a father and husband who dominated the household, regulating both Margaret and Voirrey as lower class citizens in their own house.

To imagine that any child could have constantly fooled both her parents for years with a fake voice and throwing items around the house unseen, stretches ones incredibility to the point of snapping back and causing bodily injury. Living at Doarlish Cashen, as it has often been pointed out, was primitive (no electricity, radio or telephones) and lonely. Because of this, Jim, Margaret and Voirrey were no doubt familiar with each other's personalities, habits and quirks. It doesn't seem possible that Voirrey could have faked Gef's voice for all those years and not be immediately recognized by her parents who would have told her to stop her foolishness and to go and gather the chicken's eggs.

Familiars and Boggarts

This brings us around once again to questioning on what Gef was in the first place. There are no other modern examples of anything even remotely close to a house and family being haunted by a talking, intelligent animal. As Price and Lambert wrote in *"The Haunting at Cashen's Gap,"* Gef as a Familiar or some other elemental type of entity is a possibility. Historically speaking, during the days of the Inquisitions, familiars were said to be given to witches by the devil. They were, in essence, small demons in the form of animals that would be sent out to do a witch's bidding. In animal form they can travel undetected, sometimes even invisibly, to eavesdrop on neighbors, steal items and cause sickness and death to people and livestock. In return, the witch would feed them or offer drops of her blood.

A more modern viewpoint on Familiars is that it is a spiritual helper manifest in animal form. For many it takes on the appearance of a common household pet or an animal such as a hare or weasel. There are numerous records of witches confessing to having Familiars (no doubt the result of torture), such as the 1589 Chelmsford witch trial when thirty-one people from Essexwere accused of witchcraft under the 1563 Witchcraft Act. One of the accused, Joan Prentice, described how a ferret named Bid appeared to her and said "Joan Prentice, give me thy soul." Joan refused as she believed her soul was not hers to give. After reaching an agreement, Bid said to her: "I must then have some of thy blood." Joan offered him the forefinger of her left hand and the ferret took it into his mouth and sucked blood from her finger. Not unlike when Margaret Irving placed one of her fingers into Gef's mouth, accidentally drawing blood when it was cut by his teeth.

Depending on one's religious beliefs, one man's Familiar is another man's Hob. Gef is also very reminiscent to a Tutelary spirit; guardians found in many traditions protecting people and property. Brownies fall into the category of elemental spirits that guards houses and families. These "hobs" allegedly would seek out "deserving" families that were hard-workers who had fallen on hard times and could use a helping hand. Although Brownies were known to be helpful, they could also cause considerable trouble if not fed and treated properly.

When Brownies were thought to be helping one household, neighbors would be suspicious when things would go missing from their property. The Brownie, Tomte, Nisse, or Kobold was believed to steal milk and bags of grain from other farms to take back to his home. Gef was said to steal sandwiches and other food from people around the island to bring back to the Irvings.

Claude Lecouteux, a French scholar and author, wrote a book on domestic spirits, *"The Tradition of Household Spirits."* Lecouteux uses the word "Brownie" as a blanket term to refer to house elves in many European regions. He writes that in European folklore "the dead transformed into spirits, then into sprites or Brownies, and eventually into devils." He describes haunted houses that have been recorded in French and German historical documents that he interprets as unhappy Brownies.

He writes about houses where stones are thrown about, pages of books flipping from beginning to end with lightning speed, the sound of heavy wooden shoes clumping around, items disappearing and never seen again, as well as voices being heard from thin air. In certain parts of England and Scotland, especially in marshy or isolated areas, there is a house spirit called a Boggart. It is considered to be a comparable to a Brownie, but it can be very mischievous.

A Boggart can sometimes function like a helpful Brownie, but it often displays characteristics of a poltergeist. The Boggart may do household chores, occasionally playing pranks on the family. It is also fond of bothering children, stealing their toys or keeping them awake at night. When angered, the Boggart is particularly vicious in his response, even being known to completely destroy the entire farm.

Like Gef, house spirits are shy and have a clear dislike of being seen or spied upon. There are stories of people who hid themselves in the room where they expected the house spirit to be working. But, the house spirit almost always discovers the human and leaves the premises in a huff, never to return.

Tulpa

It has been offered that Gef may have been a "Tulpa," a sentient being imagined into existence that becomes incarnate, or embodied through thoughtform. A thoughtform is a small packet of condensed psychic energy and like all energy, the thoughtform can be programmed to carry out specific tasks and/or directed to travel to a target area. They are more than just fleeting flights of subjectivity that pass through our minds and are gone…they are our creations. Thoughtforms are dependent on the people who generate the mental energy empowering them. A weak thoughtform will quickly dissipate, accomplishing nothing. Good or bad, they are expressions of human creativity.

The practice of creating a Tulpa is considered to be extremely dangerous for anyone who has not reached a high mental and spiritual degree of enlightenment and is not fully aware of the nature of the psychic forces at work in the process.

Powerful thoughtforms, when neglected can wreak havoc. Energy feeds on energy and a thoughtform that is several weeks old will have absorbed all kinds of different influences, emotions and energies from its surroundings. This might appear amusing to some, but the mutated thoughtform has often been known to reappear in the locale of its creator, only to wreak havoc, due to the outside energies it has accumulated.

Once the Tulpa is endowed with enough vitality to be capable of playing the part of a real being, it tends to free itself from its maker's control. This, say Tibetan occultists, happens nearly mechanically, just as the child, when his body is completed and able to live apart, leaves its mother's womb. Sometimes the phantom becomes a rebellious son and one hears of uncanny struggles that have taken place between magicians and their creatures, the former being severely hurt or even killed by the latter.

"Tulpas are understood as mental constructs that have achieved sentience," Dr. Veissière says. Nearly 40 percent of his respondents reported that their Tulpas "felt as real as a physical person", while 50.6 percent described them as "somewhat real...distinct from [their] own thoughts."

In Dion Fortune's book, ***Psychic Self-Defense***, she mentions a wolf spirit that was tormenting her. This wolf it turned out was nothing more than a creation of her own will. It is also an incredible example of a Tulpa, with the exception that the wolf was never bound to her will.

A Tulpa can take on any idea, shape or purpose...the more complex the purpose, the more focus and energy required. A Tulpa created with a given purpose, such as protection; will be more effective than one whose purpose is to protect, warn, or even expedite services.

Some have asked if some thoughtforms have a reality of their own, separate of the human mind...such as an elemental. Theosophists and clairvoyants Annie Besant and C. W. Leadbeater placed thoughtforms in three classifications: (1) the image of the thinker; (2) an image of a material object associated with the thought; and (3) an independent image expressing the inherent qualities of the thought. Thoughts which are of a low nature, such as anger, hate, lust, greed, and so on, create thoughtforms which are dense in color and form. Thought of a more spiritual nature tend to generate forms possessing a greater purity, clarity, and refinement.

Thoughtforms then exist in either the mental or astral plane. Each entity is created from thought. Every thought is said to generate vibrations in the aura's mental body, which assume a floating form and colors depending on the nature and intensity of the thought. These thoughtforms are usually seen by clairvoyants; and may be not only intuitively sensed by others, but actually seen as physical entities.

Taking all of this into consideration, it is not unreasonable to consider that ALL spiritual entities, not considered to be human spirits may be constructs of the human mind...astral beings, elementals, angels, deities, a talking mongoose, etc. Could this also explain other things such as cyrptid creatures along the lines of Bigfoot, lake monsters, or even UFOs? Could all of these things be creations of the world's group mind?

Thoughtforms can occur spontaneously. "Group minds" that emerge whenever a group of people concentrate on the same thought, ideas, or goals, such as a team of employees or a crowd of demonstrators. To a certain extent the group-mind possesses the group; such is seen in psychic bonding and power that coalesces in crowds, and in the synergy of a close-knit working group. Usually when the group disbands the power of the group-mind dissipates too.

In the world of high strangeness and mysteries, what makes Gef the Talking Mongoose standout is his uniqueness. After so many years, he has never reappeared...in fact, nothing even close to Gef has ever emerged to haunt a house or family. Perhaps Gef was special because his family, the Irving's and their circumstances, were special. His genesis might have come about due to situations and individuals exclusive to that moment in time and space. A brief moment of white-hot brilliance that faded once that special time and connection faded away into the night.

Like a snowflake, Gef was unique. There can never be another like him...but his memory lives on and will never truly vanish.

Photos of Gef taken by Voirrey Irving in December, 1935 using a camera provided by Harry Price.

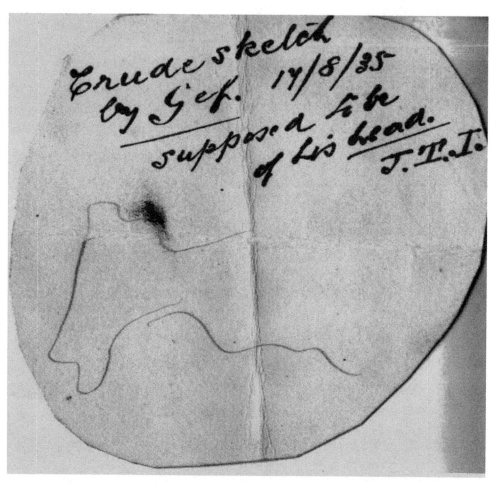

Gef provided Jim Irving with his "self-portrait" using a pencil. Notations are by Irving.

ALLEGED PHOTOGRAPH OF GEF ON TOP OF SOD HEDGE
TAKEN BY VOIRREY IRVING

HAUNTED BRITAIN

THE TALKING MONGOOSE

People who claimed to have carried on intelligent conversations in English with a furry little animal might be thought lying or mad. But surely not everyone in the locality could be mad or a liar?

It was no rat that the farmer shot in 1947 — but could it have been "Gef", the mongoose that James Irving and his wife had heard behind the walls (below) and taught to speak English more than a dozen years earlier?

Newspaper account depicting Gef being shot by the new owner of Doarlish Cashen. According to former Army Lieutenant L. Graham, who purchased the property after the death of Jim Irving, he snared and clubbed a strange black and white animal on the farm. However, when Voirrey Irving saw a photo of the dead animal, she said that its coloring was different and it was larger than Gef.

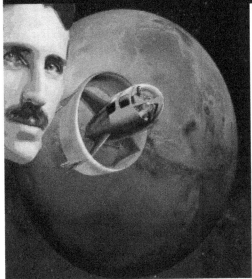

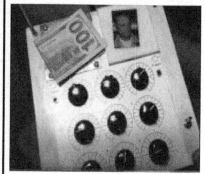
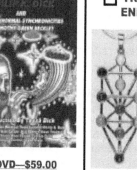

INNER LIGHT/GLOBAL COMMUNICATIONS

Published By Inner Light/Global Communications
P.O. Box 753
New Brunswick, NJ 08903

mrufo8@hotmail.com

www.conspiracyjournal.com

Made in the USA
Monee, IL
19 August 2021